Changing Minds

The History of Psychotherapy as an
Answer to Human Suffering

FRANK TALLIS

CASSELL
London and New York

Cassell
Wellington House
125 Strand
London WC2R 0BB

370 Lexington Avenue
New York
NY 10017–6550

www.cassell.co.uk

© Frank Tallis 1998

First published 1998

British Library Cataloguing-in-Publication Data
A catalogue record for this book is available from the British Library.

ISBN   0-304-70362-1 (hardback)
        0-304-70363-x (paperback)

Typeset by Textype Typesetters, Cambridge
Printed and bound in Great Britain by
Biddles Ltd, Guildford and King's Lynn

Contents

1	A Rooted Sorrow	1
2	The Excavation of the Mind	24
3	After Freud	47
4	The Exiled Mind	78
5	The Search for Meaning	106
6	The Mind Regained	131
7	Divided by a Common Language	150
	Further Reading	170
	Index	172

Know Thyself

Know then thyself, presume not God to scan;
The proper study of Mankind is Man.
Plac'd on this isthmus of a middle state,
A being darkly wise, and rudely great:
With too much knowledge for the Sceptic side,
With too much weakness for the Stoic's pride,
He hangs between; in doubt to act, or rest,
In doubt to deem himself a God, or Beast:
In doubt his Mind or Body to prefer;
Born but to die, and reas'ning but to err;
Alike in ignorance, his reason such,
Whether he thinks too little, or too much:
Chaos of Thought and Passion, all confus'd;
Still by himself abus'd, or disabus'd;
Created half to rise, and half to fall;
Great lord of all things, yet a prey to all;
Sole judge of Truth, in endless Error hurl'd:
The glory, jest, and riddle of the world!

Alexander Pope (1688–1744), *An Essay on Man*, Epistle II,
lines 1–18

CHAPTER 1

A Rooted Sorrow

'First Gods, then demi-gods, then kings, then great warriors, great lovers, then burghers and merchants and vicars and doctors and lawyers. Then social realism: you. Then irony: me. Then maniacs and murderers, tramps, mobs, rabble, flotsam, vermin.'

Martin Amis, *The Information*

Over two-and-a-half thousand years ago, Siddharta Gautama, an Indian prince born to a protected existence of great luxury, saw illness and death for the first time. He subsequently renounced the world and vowed to learn the meaning and purpose of life. After six years of wandering, during which he practised the most extreme austerities, he came across a Bodhi tree, turned towards the east and sat down to meditate. Tradition has it that seven days later, Siddharta Gautama emerged from his trance as a perfect being: the Buddha. He proclaimed, as the first of his four noble truths, that 'All life is suffering'.

At one point or another, most of us will be forced to agree with the Buddha. Whether because of a specific event, such as the death of a loved one, or a pervasive sense of meaninglessness, life will be suffered, rather than lived. Suffering, it would appear, is an unavoidable aspect of the human condition.

Religious beliefs have always protected people from the harsher realities of existence. Even death is reduced to a minor inconvenience, not more than a short sleep that precedes everlasting life; however, of late, religion appears to have stopped working. When people experience suffering, they no longer turn to God (and God's representatives) with the same degree of conviction that characterized prior ages. To embark upon a journey towards spiritual enlightenment requires at least some degree of faith, and in the twentieth century, faith has been in short supply. In fact, our faith has been slowly ebbing away over a period of nearly five hundred years.

The medieval world was a world of certainties. A world in which the existence of God was an indisputable truth. The universe kindly obliged by confirming this view; it appeared to be nothing less than an elaborate stage constructed for the benefit of mankind. Each prop and special effect seemed to underscore the human race's pre-eminent position. Every morning, the sun would reassuringly rise and trace an arc around the sky. Every evening the stars would follow. Man was in the middle of it all; something special.

It was not until the sixteenth century that the earth was wrenched from its pivotal position, by of all people, a canon of the cathedral church of Frauenberg, Nicholas Copernicus. He was born in Poland in 1473 and attended the University of Cracow. He later travelled to study in Bologna and Padua. Before releasing the final manuscript of *De Revolutionibus Orbium Coelestium*, the work which describes the heliocentric or sun-centred system, he distributed among friends and scholars an outline of his new theory called *the ballet of the planets*. This document was received with some interest; however, Copernicus decided not to publish until he was on his deathbed. He was well aware that the church would take a dim view of his discovery.

At first, nobody took much notice of *De Revolutionibus*. Resistance to the new cosmology could be explained by its inconsistency with everyday experience, its lack of classical beauty, and its unacceptable heresy against the church; however, there was also perhaps a more fundamental reason: pride. In his novel *The Information*, Martin Amis suggests that 'The history of Astronomy is the history of increasing humiliation . . . Every century we get smaller'.

Copernicus had not only succeeded in demolishing the classical universe, he had also opened the floodgates of the Renaissance. *De Revolutionibus* was based on astronomical observations, not theological argument and received wisdom. The old truths could now be doubted, and in the Renaissance, the search for truth shifted: from heaven to earth, from God to humans.

In spite of the Copernican revolution, the idea that humanity was divine handiwork persisted. Irrespective of the earth's place in the cosmos, man still seemed special. In fact, all living things appear to bear the hallmarks of design, and it was the *design* argument that sustained belief in the existence of God for many years. Like the sun's clearly observable revolutions around the earth, the extraordinary intricacy of living things and the near magical processes that guide their development constitute everyday experience. Surrounded by miracles and mystery, it was difficult to deny the existence of God; however, the design argument would prove no more resistant to scientific scrutiny than the earth-centred universe.

Charles Darwin was born in 1809, the son of a distinguished physician. While studying at Cambridge University, he abandoned his plan to become ordained and acquired a keen interest in natural history. After graduating, the young Darwin was appointed as the resident naturalist aboard the survey ship HMS *Beagle*. A subsequent five-year voyage to the South Pacific and South Atlantic prompted his first consideration of how species might evolve.

The concept of *natural selection* proved a convincing mechanism by which the development of species could be explained. The propositions that provide the cornerstones of evolutionary theory are straightforward. Organisms produce more offspring than can survive and reproduce. The organisms that survive tend to be better adapted. Parental characteristics appear in their progeny; thus, better adapted lines will survive to pass on the characteristics that give them an advantage.

Darwin suggested that complex organisms evolve by slow cumulative change. Although Darwin did not know the exact mechanism that governed fundamental changes in the appearance of organisms, we now know that these are genetic. Each genetic change is the result of a random mutation; however, the cumulative process of change, guided by natural selection, is therefore non-random. The fossil record, although marred by gaps and omissions, suggested such a process of gradual change had occurred. Moreover, given enough time, the most complex of organisms, man, could evolve.

The concept of design could now be abandoned. Without a design, there was no need to infer the presence of a designer. Humanity had simply evolved from an ape-like ancestor. In 1859, Darwin published *The Origin of Species by Means of Natural Selection, or the Preservation of Favoured Races in the Struggle for Life.* The second major blow to the foundations of religion had been struck.

Not only had the human race been ousted from the centre of the universe, but it had also slipped from its special position between beasts and angels, and had lost its footing. When Victorian families stared into the cages at London zoo, they now observed their relatives. Distant cousins. The beast was in everyone. Again, mankind had been humiliated.

As the human race has undergone successive episodes of demotion, mental illness has been a stalwart companion on the downward journey. The trajectory of descent has taken mental illness from the ethereal realms of the supernatural to the pedestrian world of brain chemistry and disease. In effect, the extreme form of human suffering that we call mental illness lost its position as a subject fit for theologians and priests and fell into the scope of interest defined by science and medicine.

The earliest evidence for a supernatural theory of mental illness is provided by archaeologists. Numerous stone age skulls have been found in which a hole had been made; some of these holes had started to heal, suggesting that many individuals actually survived this primitive operation, which was presumably executed by chipping away bone material with a sharp stone. Trephining, as the procedure is called, is believed to have provided a portal in the skull, out of which evil spirits could escape. One can assume that changes in mood and behaviour were taken as evidence for the presence of an evil spirit. The rise of civilization did nothing to moderate belief in demons as a cause of such changes. Indeed, 'demons' were considered to be a real threat within the cultural traditions of ancient Babylon, China, Egypt and Greece.

In the past, not all abnormal mental phenomena were attributed to malign influence. It is highly likely that many of the early Christian saints and visionaries were suffering from disorders such as schizophrenia; however, their unusual experiences were interpreted as divine rather than demonic. For example, descriptions of Joan of Arc suggest that she frequently listened to voices that had no human source. These were almost certainly auditory hallucinations. Nevertheless, French soldiers were willing to die for her in battle and she came to be regarded by some as a minor deity. The likes of Joan of Arc, however, were the exception. The predominant view was that unusual experiences and unusual behaviour were caused by demons, and this was a view wholly approved of by the church.

In 1484, Pope Innocent VIII resolved to rid Europe of witches. His envoys, the Dominicans James Sprenger and Henry Kraemer, gained considerable experience in the matter of hunting witches and their learning was published in the *Malleus Maleficarum* (The Witches' Hammer), an inquisitor's manual that first appeared in 1486. In this work the signs of demonic possession are described. These include a range of 'symptoms' that are clearly nothing more than delusions and hallucinations. Several chapters of the *Malleus* are replete with descriptions of women who allegedly had engaged in sexual intercourse with supernatural beings. These chapters are particularly interesting, insofar as they reveal as much to us Sprenger and Kraemer's preoccupation with female sexuality as they do the mental state of the women who were investigated. The inquisitors conclude that 'All witchcraft comes from carnal lust, which in women is insatiable.'

The fact that sudden loss of reason was considered a principal sign of possession must have sealed the fate of many unfortunates living in Europe at this time. These were mostly women who had first undergone torture and a humiliating trial. The defendant was required to enter the court backwards so that her eyes could not 'bewitch' the judge. She was usually naked and her head and genitals shaved so that no devils could conceal themselves in her hair. Records suggest that in the two centuries following publication of the *Malleus Maleficarum*, several hundred thousand innocent victims were put to death. Although it is commonly thought that most of those put to death were insane, it is very likely that a large proportion also suffered from less severe conditions such as depression, or what was then called 'melancholia'. They were ordinary women, whose mental condition had deteriorated in a social climate where misogyny was championed by both the church and the law.

Many doctors agreed with the view of the church. For example, John Lange, a distinguished fifteenth-century clinician, describes the case of a suicide on whom an autopsy was performed. A number of objects, such as pieces of wood and iron, were found in the stomach. He also describes a woman who vomited two iron nails, two needles and a 'bunch of hair'. He believed that these items had been deposited in her body by some diabolical trick and took this to be confirmation of a supernatural disease. In both cases, the possibility that these items might have been swallowed while committing or attempting suicide did not occur to him.

Even though the predominant view of mental illness was 'demonic' in origin, the early fifteenth century did not always solve the problem of abnormal behaviour by exorcism or the burning of witches at the stake. The most extraordinary example of an alternative solution was the 'ship of fools'. Certain towns would pay boatmen to deposit the insane in someone else's backyard; however, as other towns became aware of this novel social policy, ships under suspicion were prevented from leaving without their lunatic cargo. Eventually, such vessels were fated to navigate the rivers and seas of Europe, perpetually searching for a naive and unsuspecting port of call.

As the sixteenth century progressed, the practice of simply locking up the insane became increasingly common. The philosopher Michel Foucault has described the incarceration of the mentally ill as 'the great confinement'. At the end of the middle ages, leprosy retreated from western Europe. This was because, after the Crusades, links with eastern sources of infection were broken. With leprosy no longer a problem, social concern focused on the insane. Foucault suggests that the custom of excluding lepers from society (by placing them in leprosariums) provided a 'formula' for the management of those with 'deranged minds'. A lunatic could be incarcerated in much the same way as a leper.

Although the tradition of confinement gained momentum in the sixteenth century, 'madmen' had in fact been detained in special institutions for several centuries. The first of these was situated in Byzantium and was in operation in the fourth century; however, the oldest institution of this kind in Europe was London's Priory of St Mary of Bethlehem, founded in 1243. By 1403, it sheltered only 'six insane men'. An inventory of equipment made in 1398 reveals the methods of treatment in use at that time. It included 'four pairs of manacles, eleven chains of iron, six locks and keys, and two pairs of stocks'. In 1547, Henry VIII bequeathed St Mary's to the City of London, thereafter a 'hospital', to confine only the mentally ill. So dreadful were the conditions in St Mary's that its colloquial name of bedlam (the local mispronunciation of Bethlehem) has entered the English language as a byword for uproar, misrule and chaos. The insane were kept in deplorable conditions and their torment eventually became a source of entertainment for the leisured classes. As late as the nineteenth century it was possible to buy admission tickets for bedlam in order to watch the 'amusing' antics of the most disturbed inmates. At one time, the hospital attracted more tourists than the Tower of London! Similar atrocities were to be found on the continent. For example, Vienna boasted a 'Lunatic's Tower', constructed in 1784 in a manner that allowed the public to view the unfortunate occupants as if they were animals in a zoo.

The early 'asylums', which in actuality provided anything but asylum, were still treating patients as though they were possessed. Chains and punitive methods of restraint were employed, most probably to quell the rebellious spirit of the demon, even if his presence was not openly acknowledged. A patient might be strapped to a chair or made to stand in a wooden box no larger than a coffin for several weeks. Even drowning and drawing near fatal amounts of blood were viewed as 'treatments'.

The demise of demonology, and its subsequent legacy of torture and witch burning, occurred when mental illness began to be viewed as human suffering; a painful 'state of mind' that might be ameliorated by providing compassionate care and support. During the French revolution, Philippe Pinel was put in the charge of La Bicêtre, a large asylum in Paris. 'The mentally sick,' observed Pinel, 'far from being guilty people deserving of punishment are sick people whose miserable state deserves all the consideration that is due to suffering humanity. One should try with the most simple methods to restore their reason.' He removed the chains from the inmates and attempted to provide genuine asylum instead of confinement. By treating the disturbed as suffering human beings, he expelled the demons of the medieval world. Not surprisingly, the mental condition of those in his care improved.

About the same time as Pinel, a wealthy merchant Quaker in England, William Tuke, was appalled by the conditions he observed in the York Asylum. The Society of Friends pledged to form their own institution which became known as the York Retreat. This building was situated in a country estate and residents lived in a quiet religious atmosphere. Tuke shared Pinel's vision of compassion and care, and as in France, many seemingly intractable cases of 'melancholy' and 'madness' showed signs of improvement.

Thus, by the eighteenth century the suffering that we now call mental illness was ascribed to the 'human condition' rather than the intervention of supernatural forces; however, the introduction and endorsement of varieties of 'pastoral care' still implied distress arising in 'troubled souls'. The idea that melancholy and madness might be caused by a diseased brain was yet to be firmly established. Of course, when this idea gained currency, suffering of this kind was perceived explicitly as a type of illness. The process of demotion was complete. The demons, priests and humanitarians left the stage to make way for the doctor.

The doctor was in fact always present, pacing in the wings. His late entry in this drama is attributable to the fact that, until recently, what he had to say about mental illness was no more informed than the opinion of a demonologist. In fact, in most cases, the doctor had a less cohesive intellectual framework within which to understand extreme suffering and abnormal behaviour. For example, the seventeenth-century physician, John Seldon, reported treating a 'melancholic' who believed that he 'had two devils in his head' by giving him a piece of card to hang around his neck and urging him to eat less. Apparently, the treatment was successful; an outcome undoubtedly attributable to the melancholic's faith in his doctor rather than the inherent value of the method. Seldon had little to say about the rationale that guided his choice of treatment or the mechanisms that led to his patient's recovery. Before any authoritative statement could be made about the treatment of mental illness from a medical point of view, it was necessary to specify a physical cause (such as a chemical imbalance in the body). For doctors, the physical cause of mental illness proved to be as elusive as the Holy Grail.

The idea that abnormal mental phenomena could be caused by physical problems was first suggested by the Greek physician Hippocrates in the third century BC; however, it was not until the mid-nineteenth century that any evidence was forthcoming that would support Hippocrates' contention that disturbed minds were the result of disturbed brains. By 1825, doctors understood that certain symptoms had a tendency to occur together. As such, they were able to provide a fairly reliable diagnosis. The term *general paresis* was employed to describe a pattern of mental and physical deterioration affecting people in the middle and later years of life. The most disturbing of the mental symptoms was the presence of delusions, mostly of a grandiose nature. It had long been recognized that some patients with paresis had a medical history featuring the venereal disease syphilis. The mechanism that might link the two conditions became apparent when Pasteur discovered microbes in the 1860s and 1870s. In 1906, Fritz Schaudinn isolated *Treponema pallidum*, the thin, corkscrew microbe that causes syphilis and, after a period of dormancy, general paresis. Here then was a physical cause of mental anguish, a material demon.

The branch of medicine that seeks to understand and treat mental illness is psychiatry. The discovery of the link between syphilis and insanity suggested that all mental problems might one day be understood in terms of specific diseases that affected the brain. This was a triumph for 'reductionism' (the guiding principle of all scientific enquiry), which suggests that the best way to understand a phenomenon is to redefine it at a more basic level. Thus, the whole is understood in terms of its constituent parts. After the mystery of general paresis had been unravelled, psychiatry was well placed to become a reductionist discipline; it was a legitimate branch of medical science that could establish clear connections between mental illness and biological abnormalities; however, just as 'biological pyschiatry' was becoming established, something happened in Paris that would halt and eventually reverse the reductionist trend. Indeed, biological psychiatry would not recover from this setback for another sixty years.

The medical texts and fiction written in Europe in the latter half of the nineteenth century give the impression that the continent was seething with *hysterical* women. They were sensitive and fragile, swooning under the slightest duress, and prone to the development of dramatic symptoms such as paralysis. An arm or a leg might suddenly become completely insensitive, perplexing the examining physicians who would find no evidence of disease or deterioration. The great Parisian neurologist, Jean-Martin Charcot, content to ride the tide of medical optimism, believed firmly in a biological cause. A 'weak' nervous system perhaps? However, some students of his had been experimenting with hypnotism, a technique developed by the Austrian physician and showman, Anton Mesmer. Charcot's students hypnotized a healthy woman and by making certain suggestions, were able to reproduce some of the main symptoms of *hysteria*. The master was called to examine the 'patient' and he was wholly deceived. Here then, was a healthy brain that had been encouraged to show the symptoms of hysteria. Charcot became less certain of a biological cause and became interested in exploring hysteria from a psychological perspective.

Charcot was an impressive figure. He was not only one of the finest minds of his age, but also a charismatic performer. A famous painting by André Brouillet, *La Leçon clinique du Dr Charcot*, shows Charcot 'demonstrating' a hysterical woman to an audience in the Salpêtrière. They are rapt and quite literally on the edge of their seats. Indeed, at that time, it must have been an extraordinary sight to see symptoms such as hysterical paralysis being created and removed by suggestion alone. In one such audience, in 1885, sat a young Viennese doctor. When he wasn't being astonished by Charcot's histrionics, he persevered with his temporary backroom job; a microscopic study of children's brains in Charcot's laboratory. After seeing Charcot's performances, he would return to the microscope with ever decreasing enthusiasm.

In January 1886, Charcot invited the young man to a party in his palatial home. The hopeful young doctor was so unsure of himself that he took a dose of cocaine before leaving his rooms. He was relieved when the evening ended. He wrote to his fiancée saying that he had managed, with the help of the cocaine, to get by without making a fool of himself. When he returned to Vienna that year, he translated a volume of Charcot's lectures. He then developed a method of treating psychological problems that involved simply 'talking' to patients; however, it wasn't until 1896 that he gave it a name. He called the method 'psychoanalysis', the first example of what came to be known as psychotherapy. His ideas about the true nature of man were less than flattering, and many would argue that his writings completed the process of humiliating descent started by Copernicus and accelerated by Darwin. Needless to say, his rising star completely eclipsed Charcot. The young, nervous, cocaine-dependent doctor was Sigmund Freud.

The year 1886 was an eventful one for Freud. When he returned to Vienna from Paris, he married, and set up in private practice as a consultant in nervous diseases. He published some important academic articles on the nervous system and became an authority on cerebral palsies of children. Whereas most in his position would have been satisfied to rest on their laurels, Freud pressed on. Although he remained interested in diseases of the nervous system, his attention began to shift from the brain to the mind.

In 1888, he began working with his friend, Dr Joseph Breuer. Breuer was Freud's senior by 14 years; however, their relationship was, at least in the early stages, very close. Breuer was something of a kindly uncle. In 1882, Breuer had told Freud about an interesting case that he was then treating, an educated, creative and intelligent 21-year-old woman who had spent much of her time nursing a terminally ill father. She had exhibited a range of hysterical symptoms. These included headaches, loss of hearing, coughing, squinting, impaired vision, and paralysis of several parts of her body. In addition, she would sometimes lose the ability to talk properly, or would be able only to talk in a foreign language. She had suffered from dramatic mood swings and for extended periods of time had stopped eating or drinking; however, her most dramatic symptom was lapsing into a dream-like state in which she had suffered from terrifying supernatural hallucinations. These hallucinations occurred only during the day. No physical cause for these symptoms could be found. If she had lived in the fifteenth century, she would almost certainly have been burned as a witch.

Breuer had visited his patient almost every evening, because it was at this time that she would spontaneously enter an altered state of mind similar to a hypnotic trance and begin to utter the words 'tormenting, tormenting'. If a phrase that she had spoken earlier in the day while hallucinating was repeated at this point, she would begin to tell a story. Her stories were always sad and reminded Breuer of those written by Hans Christian Andersen. When each story was finished, the young woman would become calm, cheerful and lucid. She coined a term to describe this procedure. It is often wrongly attributed to Freud and is now used to describe most forms of psychotherapy: 'the talking cure'. She also called the procedure, rather whimsically, 'chimney sweeping', which for fairly obvious reasons did not catch on in quite the same way. Unfortunately, the effects of the talking cure were short-lived. The following day she would be agreeable; however, on the second day she would become increasingly moody. By the third evening she had usually resumed her private battle with hallucinations that had once again begun to invade her waking hours.

Breuer recognized that the altered state of mind that the young woman entered at night was similar to hypnosis and subsequently began hypnotizing the patient himself. He had asked her questions about her symptoms and found that each one of them was in some way related to a forgotten event that had occurred while she had been nursing her dying father. For example, her squint and impaired vision were associated with an occasion when she had been crying and could not see properly. It was as though traumatic memories and distressing feelings had been buried in some inaccessible part of her mind from where they were able to exert a powerful influence. This process of 'burying' memories was eventually described as *repression*. When these important events and feelings were retrieved under hypnosis, the young woman's symptoms disappeared. Summarizing these findings, Breuer wrote: 'Each individual symptom in this complicated case was taken separately in hand; all the occasions on which it had appeared were described in reverse order . . . going back to the event which had led to its first appearance. When this had been described the symptom was permanently removed.' Naturally, Breuer concluded that these repressed and traumatic memories were actually causing her symptoms. This was a breakthrough. Charcot had merely demonstrated that hysterical symptoms could be created and removed under hypnosis. His work had not revealed the processes that governed the development of hysterical symptoms in 'real life'. For the first time, the symptoms of hysteria were being understood in a meaningful way. Furthermore, the links being made between the causes and symptoms had little to do with the brain and the nervous system. The causes were purely psychological. In *Macbeth*, Shakespeare's flawed hero asks the doctor attending his disturbed wife to perform a seemingly impossible task: 'Canst thou not minister to a mind diseas'd, pluck from the memory a rooted sorrow.' Breuer had done exactly that. A rooted sorrow had been plucked from the depths of memory.

It was not until Freud had started his own private practice that he was in a position to experiment with Breuer's technique. He hypnotized his patients and helped them to retrieve significant memories and feelings that had been repressed, and perhaps to his initial surprise, observed improvement in his patients. Once Freud had collected a series of case studies, he urged Breuer to collaborate with him on a work summarizing their discoveries. The work was called *Studies on Hysteria* and the key case reported was Breuer's 21-year-old woman. In order to protect her identity, Breuer called her Anna O. This enigmatic name would be forever remembered as the first patient ever to receive psychotherapy.

Feminist writers have made much of Anna O. Some have pondered why Breuer concealed the identity of his patient by choosing this name in particular. It has been suggested that the palindromic 'Anna' represents the divided female psyche, while the O implicates the madness of Ophelia. The O or circle is also, of course, an ancient symbol for the female genitalia. Whether these considerations entered Breuer's mind or not we shall never know; however, of greater interest is the fact that we now know who she was: Bertha Pappenheim, a friend, in fact, of Freud's wife. In later life, Pappenheim became a prominent social worker, a reformer and a feminist activist. She translated Mary Wollstonecraft's *Vindication of the Rights of Women*, wrote a play called *Women's Rights*, and was one of the founder members of the German League of Jewish Women.

Such achievements strongly suggest that Breuer's treatment was successful. Indeed, it would be impossible to imagine how such a catalogue of achievements could have been accomplished had Pappenheim's original symptoms persisted; however, the treatment was not an unequivocal success. When Breuer wrote up the case of Anna O. for his joint publication with Freud, he admits to having 'suppressed a large number of quite interesting details'. In fact, Bertha Pappenheim had fallen in love with Breuer. The treatment ended when she experienced stomach cramps, and imagined that she was giving birth to Breuer's child. At this point, Breuer deserted his patient. As far as he was concerned, he had done as much as he could. He referred Pappenheim to a colleague, and was more or less happy to forget the whole business. Had it not been for Freud, the talking cure would have been entirely forgotten. In 1932, some fifty years after these events, Freud wrote that when Anna O. had declared her phantom pregnancy, Breuer had 'held the key in his hand' and had chosen to drop it. It is because Freud picked up the key, and not Breuer, that he is remembered as the father of psychotherapy. The 'key' was to do with sexuality, and Breuer, the middle-aged, respectable physician, was distinctly unhappy about it. Ironically, Freud might well have expressed his ideas about the true origins of hysteria by paraphrasing the authors of the *Malleus Maleficarum*: 'All suffering comes from carnal lust, which in women is repressed.'

In addition to the case of Anna O. there are four other cases described in the *Studies on Hysteria*. The third of these, Katharina, is not so much a case study as a journal entry. Freud describes walking in the Alps in order to escape the medical world and neurotic patients when he is unexpectedly accosted by a young woman. Having previously discovered that he was a doctor, she had pursued him in order to request a consultation. She aroused his curiosity by disclosing her symptoms. These included breathlessness, dizziness, a crushing sensation on the chest, and a recurrent hallucination of 'an awful face' near her own. Freud rather humorously remarked: 'So there I was with the neuroses once again . . . interested to find that neuroses could flourish in this way at a height of 6000 feet.' He was unable to resist 'analysing' her immediately. During their short conversation, Freud discovered that her anxiety symptoms were the result of a sexual trauma that occurred in her early adolescence. Her lascivious uncle (whom she was to discover some years later in bed with her cousin) had attempted to have intercourse with her while she was asleep. She awoke 'feeling his body' against her and left the room is a distressed state. Freud hoped that these disclosures would relieve Katharina's symptoms. After this strange meeting, he never saw her again. The case study is intriguing insofar as it demonstrates that even when on holiday in the Alps, Freud would not miss an opportunity to gather evidence that would support his burgeoning ideas on the sexual origin of hysterical and neurotic symptoms. Some thirty years after the first publication of the *Studies on Hysteria* Freud added a footnote to the text. In order to disguise Katharina's identity he had modified her story. The man who had tried to sexually abuse her was not her uncle, but her father. It was a fact that, at the time, Freud did not realize was of great significance.

Even as Freud and Breuer were collaborating, irreconcilable differences of opinion had begun to emerge. Freud believed that mechanisms existed for the preservation of 'peace of mind', which served to keep forbidden or disturbing sexual feelings out of awareness. It was the repression of sexual feelings, more than any other type, that would be likely to produce hysterical and neurotic (that is, anxiety-related) symptoms. He did not, at this stage, believe that all manifestations of hysteria were attributable to repressed sexual impulses, but he was convinced that matters sexual should be given considerably more emphasis than Breuer was prepared to concede. Aware of Breuer's reservations about the role of sexuality, Freud wrote in the final section of the *Studies on Hysteria*: 'fresh points of view have forced themselves on my mind. These have led to what is in part at least a different . . . interpretation of the factual material known to me . . . It would be unfair if I were to try to lay too much responsibility for this development upon my honoured friend Dr Josef Breuer.' Freud had also begun to modify Breuer's therapeutic procedure. He became swiftly disaffected with hypnosis as a therapeutic tool and instead preferred his patients to simply lie down and talk, saying anything that came into their heads. He called the method *free association*.

Freud became increasingly frustrated with Breuer. It seemed to him that his senior partner just wasn't accepting the evidence. Breuer would support Freud in public when he espoused a *sexual theory* of hysteria, then privately explain that he didn't believe a word of it. At a later date Breuer would write: 'the plunging into sexuality in theory and practice is not to my taste.' Clearly, the generation gap was just wide enough to admit a difference in attitude towards sex; however, Freud's insistence on the importance of sexuality was disturbing Breuer for more personal reasons.

Breuer and Bertha Pappenheim had established a close, almost collaborative relationship. Pappenheim's intellectual contribution to the process of treatment was, in truth, as important as Breuer's. He liked her and, perhaps, when he returned home to Frau Breuer, after an evening of 'Arabian

Nights'-style entertainment, his domestic situation seemed dull by contrast. Breuer's description of Pappenheim's personal attributes is revealing: 'She had great poetic and imaginative gifts, which were under the control of a sharp and critical common sense . . . One of her essential character traits was sympathetic kindness. Even during her illness she herself was greatly assisted by being able to look after a number of poor, sick people . . .' Did his affection for Pappenheim deepen to the extent that his resolve to keep a professional distance began to falter? So much so, that when Freud insisted on the importance of sexual impulses, the image of Bertha Pappenheim, clutching her abdomen, claiming to be giving birth to his child, was still all too vivid in his mind? It was all very embarrassing. He didn't want to be reminded; but Freud just wouldn't let the subject rest. They stopped talking to each other and Freud continued on his own.

As Freud continued to practise, he discovered that most of his patients could recall an episode of sexual seduction. Many of these had occurred not during adolescence, as in the case of Katharina, but in infancy. The perpetrator of the seduction was usually the parent of the opposite sex. At first, Freud considered these reports to be accurate; however, he later began to have serious doubts. Was it really possible that the fine, upstanding gentlemen of Vienna were sexually abusing and subsequently traumatizing their own daughters? After some consideration Freud revised his ideas and suggested that these traumatic memories could not be real. He employed the term *screen memories* to describe them and concluded that they represented the residue of early sexual fantasies. This notion eventually led him to suggest that children, even very young children, have sexual feelings.

The child is of course a symbol of innocence and purity. In Freud's time, the prevailing view of children had been shaped by the romantic excesses of the Victorian novelists, most notably Charles Dickens. They were pure souls, untainted by the world; however, for Freud, children were merely individuals who had not yet been subject to the civilizing influence of society. To look at the mind of a child was to look at humanity raw. The fundamental Darwinian instincts to survive and successfully reproduce were already active, influencing infant feelings and fantasies. Later in his life, Freud would write: 'young children are amoral and possess no internal inhibitions against their impulses striving for pleasure.' The beast had invaded the nursery.

In their early case studies Breuer and Freud had revealed that a major cause of mental illness was the presence of distressing memories that had been repressed, or buried, in an inaccessible part of the mind. This locked 'basement' of mental life came to be called *the unconscious*. Hypnotism and free association had been useful tools, allowing Freud to gain access to unconscious material. Patients could lie down on the now famous analyst's couch and be encouraged to remember key events; however, the unconscious mind protects its secrets. Were it not so possessive, its hidden treasures could be retrieved by a simple act of will. Freud had noticed that the most important memories were the least accessible. They *resisted* enquiry. Therefore, a more potent tool than either hypnotism or free association was required.

He began what in psychoanalytic mythology is represented as an epic voyage, an odyssey for the modern world. It was a journey undertaken, not over land or tempestuous seas, but inwards, to explore the completely unknown country of the unconscious mind. Freud initiated his own 'self-analysis'. In a gesture bordering on the surreal he put himself on the couch. The method that allowed him to gain entry into his own 'underworld' was the examination of the content of his own dreams. For Freud, dreams were like ciphers, coded messages broadcast in the night. He set about breaking the code and even before this work was completed, he was convinced that he had made a breakthrough of profound importance. He later wrote: 'The interpretation of dreams is in fact the royal road to a knowledge of the unconscious; it is the securest foundation of psychoanalysis . . .' Copernicus had waited until he was on his deathbed before publishing *De Revolutionibus*. Darwin too had resisted publication of *The Origin of Species* for 15 years. In the tradition set by these illustrious predecessors, Freud did not publish immediately. He waited for several years before finally collecting his ideas together in *The Interpretation of Dreams*; a most uncharacteristic act of restraint for a man convinced that he was about to change the contemporary view of the mind. The work was published in 1899, but was dated 1900. It provided a new outlook for a new century.

Freud knew that he had written an important work; however, the academic community received his book with extraordinary reticence. Six hundred copies of *The Interpretation of Dreams* were printed. It took eight years to sell them all. In the first six weeks, 123 copies were sold. Only 228 more were sold over the next two years. It has since become a worldwide best seller. Towards the end of his life, Freud maintained that this book contained his most valuable discoveries. It explained the mechanisms that govern the content of dreams, and confirmed his earlier speculations on the nature of the unconscious mind. Yet more important was the apparent confirmation of the role of repressed sexual urges (and particularly those dating back to childhood) in the formation of symptoms.

Although Freud always claimed to be an objective scientist, at times he was anything but objective. By placing himself on the couch, he had allowed his own feelings and experiences to bias his thinking. In fact, an idea that eventually became the cornerstone of psychoanalytic theory, the *Oedipus complex*, was very much influenced by Freud's personal psychology. That Freud felt sexually attracted to his own mother is well documented. In 1897, when undertaking his own self-analysis, Freud was able to retrieve memories of her that had previously been repressed. Writing to his close friend, Wilhelm Fliess, he described an overnight train journey which probably took place when he was about four years old. On this journey his 'libido toward matrem had awakened' when he had the 'opportunity of seeing her nudam'. This fleeting and forbidden glimpse of naked flesh was destined to influence the subsequent development of psychoanalysis for several decades.

Freud's sexual feelings towards his mother were complemented by jealous feelings towards his father. These emotions, arising in the context of early family relationships, seemed to resonate more strongly on account of the existence of works such as Sophocles' *Oedipus Rex* and Shakespeare's *Hamlet*. Freud mulled over these connections: Oedipus, the

King. Oedipus, who unknowingly killed his father and married his mother. Hamlet, terrified by the ghost of his father, and preoccupied with images of Gertrude, lying in 'the rank sweat of an enseamed bed . . . honeying and making love'. Did these works have such universal appeal, because they stirred a forgotten and forbidden memory? A universal memory, a fragment of which he had uncovered during his own self-analysis?

The Oedipus complex provided a framework within which Freud could embed and make sense of many of his clinical observations, particularly the 'screen memories' of infant seduction. Freud believed that all children pass through a phase of development in which they are attracted to the parent of the opposite sex. Forbidden feelings of this kind were repressed, and if not 'worked through' or resolved by adulthood, could result in the production of neurotic symptoms. Although many found this notion absurd (not least of all some of his early followers), he maintained that the Oedipus complex was the most significant of all rooted sorrows.

By 1905, Freud had already laid the theoretical foundations of psychoanalysis. Concepts such as repression, the unconscious, infant sexuality and the Oedipus complex promised to completely revolutionize the way doctors thought about the mind. Only 17 years earlier, when Freud was conducting his initial investigations with Breuer, the recommended treatment for hysteria and neurotic problems was *electrotherapy*. This involved a weak electric current being passed through the skin and underlying muscle tissue. In developing psychoanalysis, a method of treating psychological problems that involved simply 'talking' about experiences, memories and dreams, Freud was ostensibly in opposition to those who favoured a biological approach. Clearly, human suffering could not be eradicated by means of a weak electric current! As such, it might be argued that Freud had began to dignify human suffering. It meant something; however, the general framework that Freud developed to understand human behaviour and motivation as a whole was completely undignified. He compared himself to Copernicus and Darwin.

This comparison is usually interpreted as an arrogant assertion of his scientific credentials; but it is clear from his works that he saw Copernicus and Darwin as individuals who had confronted the narcissism of the human race. His own ideas would completely shatter any vestigial delusions of grandeur.

It is a curious paradox that the father of psychotherapy was, fundamentally, a biological determinist. That is to say, he was convinced that the ultimate determinants of human behaviour could be located in the body and, in particular, the nervous system. Although psychological problems might arise from experience, the drives that propel men and women through life are essentially biological and primitive. Thus, he gave special emphasis to basic instincts such as sex and aggression.

The Freudian view of mankind is, in fact, not only primitive, but also unremittingly bleak. Civilization is nothing more than a thin veneer; so thin, that it barely contains the true, animal nature of mankind. Manners and policy, wit and propriety, hide a seething maelstrom of primitive desires. Although any individual is capable of remarkable achievements in science and art, he or she can be easily disturbed by the repressed preoccupations of infancy: sucking at the breast, deriving pleasure from defecating, wishing to kill in a fit of explosive anger and rage. According to Freud, human beings are limited by their evolutionary legacy; a brutal legacy that is written in the symbolic language of the unconscious and inscribed in every fibre of the nervous system. As a species, we are ill-prepared for noble aspirations and enlightenment. When we express noble aspirations, we are merely pretending. The social psychiatrist J. A. C. Brown writes: 'Freud believed in the person as a social atom requiring community only as a means to the satisfaction of his needs; in a primary hostility so strong that only sheer necessity or common hatred directed elsewhere could join people in love.'

It is an extraordinary fact that against a background of biological determinism and pessimism, Freud developed a method for changing minds, and a system designed to relieve mental suffering. It is even more extraordinary that a man who believed that the human mind was little more than a covered cesspit should spend his life patiently listening to the troubles of others in the hope that he might ease their pain. Sadly, the twentieth century appears to have confirmed Freud's bleak vision of humanity. As a Jew, he was of course obliged to flee Vienna just before the Second World War. His books had already been publicly burned on the streets of Berlin.

Freud described himself as 'a godless Jew'. He was a materialist who was destined to make mankind face an empty cosmos while at the same time exposing and laying bare the primitive foundations of so-called civilized society. Like the Buddha, Freud believed that suffering was unavoidable. He also believed that religion had evolved as a kind of defence mechanism. Belief in a benign God could be viewed as a method of preserving the principal delusion of infancy: *I am special*. Belief in God also suggested the existence of an absolute system of values, which served to contain man's primitive and violent nature and shore up societal institutions such as the law. Although Freud wrote that eventually man would be able to divest himself of the necessary fiction of religion, he did not feel that contemporary man had sufficient wisdom and maturity to meet the challenge.

Copernicus and Darwin shook the foundations of the religious world-view, leaving the human race unprotected in an infinite and cold place. In the new cosmos, the choiring angels have been replaced by a vacuum whose silence and capacity to extinguish life is infinite. Although Freud pointed out that human beings are poorly equipped to deal with existence in a godless universe, he did more than just outline problems, he suggested solutions; and his main solution was to understand the nature of suffering from a human perspective. He rejected the spiritual solutions. Instead, he favoured *insight*.

The last lines of the *Studies on Hysteria* reveal the unlikely common ground shared by the Buddha and Freud. He suggests that his patients often expressed the following objection to his treatment: 'you tell me yourself that my illness is probably connected with my circumstances and the events of my life. You cannot alter these in any way. How do you propose to help me, then?' Freud's reply was straightforward: 'No doubt fate would find it easier than I do to relieve you of your illness. But you will be able to convince yourself that much will be gained if we succeed in transforming your hysterical misery into common unhappiness.' The goal then was not to remove suffering, but to make it easier to bear. To convert misery into *common unhappiness*. The alchemy that might bring about this modest transformation was psychotherapy; a secular response to the problems of the human condition.

CHAPTER 2

The Excavation of the Mind

'Of this, at least, I feel assured, that there is no such thing as
forgetting possible to the mind.'

Thomas De Quincey, *Confessions of an English Opium Eater*

Eight years after the publication of the *Studies on Hysteria*, a
number of young doctors declared a keen interest in Freud's
methods of treatment. They would meet with him every
Wednesday night, at his house, Bergasse 19, to discuss the
newly discovered discipline of psychoanalysis. This informal
club, containing no more than a handful of members, became
the nucleus of what would one day be called the Vienna
Psychoanalytic Society. Freud's fame, even after the publication
of what he considered to be a major work, *The Interpretation of
Dreams*, was strictly limited. His ideas had not spread very much
further than his own neighbourhood. By the 1920s, however,
he was well on the way to becoming an icon. His name and his
photograph (showing a rather serious, elderly looking
gentleman, with penetrating eyes) were known to millions all
over the world. In less than twenty years, he had risen from
relative obscurity to international celebrity.

, In 1925, speaking at the opening ceremony of the Hebrew
University in Jerusalem, the English statesman, Lord Balfour,
linked Freud with two Nobel Prize winners: Bergson and
Einstein. In Balfour's opinion, these three Jewish men were
responsible for the most profound developments in modern
thought. The American psychologist, William McDougall,
observed that many of Freud's technical terms had 'become
embodied in the popular slang of both America and England'.
So great was Freud's influence that even Hollywood demanded

'a piece of the action'. The film magnate, Samuel Goldwyn, asked Freud for a script! On 24 January 1925, The *New York Times* carried an extraordinary headline: 'Freud Rebuffs Goldwyn. Viennese Psychoanalyst is Not Interested in Motion Picture Offer.' Freud had responded to the Hollywood invitation with a one sentence reply: 'I do not intend to see Mr Goldwyn.'

Summarizing the enormity of Freud's influence, the writer Stefan Zweig wrote to his friend: 'I believe, that the revolution you have called forth in the psychological and philosophical and the whole moral structure of our world greatly outweighs the merely therapeutic part of your discoveries. For today all the people who know nothing about you, every human being of 1930, even the one who has never heard the name psychoanalyst, is already indirectly dyed through and through by your transformation of souls.'

How can Freud's swift ascent be explained? In a world that had received his magnum opus with indifference, how was it that Freud had managed to secure a position as one of the twentieth century's intellectual giants? One possibility is that the world had been waiting for psychoanalysis to happen. Although it took many years for the ideas in *The Interpretation of Dreams* to be recognized, the prospect of developing a better understanding of the workings of the mind had been mooted for some time. Indeed, throughout the nineteenth century, café society intellectuals were discussing concepts that would eventually be united under the banner of psychoanalysis. By 1900, the existence of an unconscious mental life and the meaning of dreams were by no means novel topics of conversation. The poet and essayist, Ralph Waldo Emerson, suggested that in the nineteenth century 'the mind had become aware of itself'. Freud was carried into the twentieth century on a wave of interest that had been gathering momentum for nearly a hundred years. In retrospect, Freud's conquest of the intellectual world was probably assisted by that great icon maker, good timing.

Nevertheless, even when historical and cultural factors are taken into account, Freud's ascent is still a remarkable phenomenon. The expansion of the Wednesday-night club from a handful of admirers to a worldwide movement in less than twenty years seems to suggest that Freud's ideas were meaningful to a very large number of people. The impetus conferred by the psychological preoccupations of the preceding century might explain the widespread acceptance of Freud's ideas; however, a benign Zeitgeist fails to explain their subsequent longevity. This is an important point, because since the 1920s academics have been vying for a position in a veritable gallery of iconoclasts whose sole intention has been to raze the edifice of Freudian psychology to the ground. This outpouring of critical publications has proved virtually inextinguishable and remains a lively tradition in academic life today; however, in spite of relentless hostility, Freud's ideas have withstood generations of assault. His works can be found in almost any bookshop and his cultural significance is beyond question. This is quite extraordinary, because even an amateur adversary could not wish for an easier target. At first sight, many of Freud's ideas seem frankly absurd and he made few efforts during his lifetime to make them more palatable. The fact that Freud is still so widely read suggests that embedded in his prolific output are insights of such power and significance that the human race is willing to forgive him his predilection for extremity and excess.

What then were Freud's ideas? What did he have to say that inspired reverence in some and ridicule in others? Apart from a number of early medical works, Freud wrote approximately three-and-a-half million words on the subject of psychoanalysis. He revised his theories throughout his life and often changed his mind with respect to what he thought should be considered important. Moreover, after changing his mind, he rarely gave a full explanation of what that change meant in relation to the status of earlier writings. His numerous volumes, articles and extensive correspondence leave stark contradictions unresolved. Indeed, some of his later ideas were not elaborated, giving the impression of 'work in progress'.

In the following, an attempt is made to give a description of key Freudian concepts. It should be noted that little consideration is given to the development of ideas over time. Therefore, the present summary represents more or less what

Freud had come to believe by the end of his life. 'More or less', because certain inconsistencies have never been resolved, nor lacunae adequately filled.

Freud's main contributions can be divided into four areas. Firstly, he described the 'architecture' and 'machinery' of the mind. That is to say, he introduced ideas that made it easier to discuss what the mind 'looks like' and 'how it works'. Secondly, he described how minds change over time. In other words, he gave an account of growth or *normal development*. Thirdly, he described how normal development can go wrong. In doing so, he suggested an explanation for the origins of mental illness. Finally, he described a method of treatment: psychoanalysis, a procedure for 'fixing' minds. Each of these contributions will be dealt with in turn.

Freud believed that the mind contains energies that, broadly speaking, obey the laws of physics. One force might be converted into another; two forces might work against each other to produce a third; and so on. Energies can build up, but eventually must be released. The model of the mind that Freud developed is often referred to as 'psychodynamic', thus acknowledging a debt to *dynamics*, the branch of nineteenth-century physics concerned with the interplay of forces. The mental energies contained in the mind are channelled in order to serve particular purposes by *instincts*, or *drives*.

Any general psychological theory must have something to say about motivation. What 'drives' human beings? Clearly, human beings are driven by many things; however, Freud believed that all human behaviour could ultimately be explained with recourse to just two fundamental instincts or drives: *Eros*, the erotic, or life instinct, and *Thanatos* the destructive, or death instinct.

Few people would argue with the idea that much of human behaviour is concerned with survival. To posit that human beings have an instinct that lends itself to preserving life is hardly controversial. Indeed, all living creatures appear to show a variety of behaviours that serve what we might choose to describe as the 'survival instinct'; however, Eros is, in all but name, the sex drive. The term employed to describe the energy of the life instinct is *libido*, and in almost all of Freud's writing, libido has little to do with the preservation of life as such, but rather with the achievement of sexual satisfaction. The distinction between the instinct and its energy is rather confusing and in most of Freud's writings the term libido is most easily understood if simply thought of as the sex drive.

Freud introduced the death instinct to explain a range of destructive or aggressive behaviours usually seen in clinical practice, for example, suicide, risk taking or self-injury; however, the influence of the death instinct can be deduced in everyday life by the presence of self-defeating decisions and morbid preoccupations. Freud linked the idea of the death instinct with aggression; however, the links between Thanatos and aggression are by no means clear. It is perhaps easier to think of aggression as an independent attribute which, like the urge to reproduce, has been selected by evolution to ensure the survival of the species.

Freud believed that sexual energy 'builds up' in the body. When this happens, the mental consequences include an increased awareness of sexual wishes or desires. This build-up of libido motivates the individual to seek sexual experiences that can satisfy desires and provide a channel for the release of energy. Although Freud knew nothing of sex hormones, these chemicals are most probably the physical basis of the sex drive. Freud has been severely criticized for giving the sex drive special emphasis; however, to do so is entirely consistent with Darwin's theory of evolution. Natural selection has ensured the preservation of the species by favouring those with a strong urge to reproduce.

According to Freud, mental life takes place on three different levels which he described as *conscious, preconscious,* and *unconscious.* These different levels of 'awareness' can be understood by employing a 'searchlight' analogy. Everything illuminated within its beam can be said to represent the contents of the conscious mind. Some objects are within reach; however, when unlit, they remain outside awareness. They can be retrieved into consciousness if the searchlight is turned on them. Everything that is accessible or within range corresponds with the preconscious. There are some objects, however, that are simply too far away to be illuminated by the beam.

Everything beyond the searchlight's range is analogous to the unconscious mind.

In addition to specifying three levels of consciousness, Freud also partitioned the mind into three sections or '*agencies*': the *id*, the *ego* and the *superego*. They are described as 'agencies' because they are not merely different parts of the mind. Each has a function or role. The boundaries between the id, ego and superego are imprecise. Indeed, Freud suggested that these regions of the mind are best thought of as 'areas of colour melting into one another' as exemplified in modern art.

The id is entirely inaccessible to the conscious mind; however, it is constantly 'striving' to satisfy the basic drives that arise in the body. Thus, the id will influence mental life in such a way as to favour the reduction of any tension associated with a build-up of libido. It can be thought of as the wellspring of desire. Indeed, Freud suggested that the id houses 'the passions'.

The mind of a newborn child has no divisions. It is comprised only of the id. The infant simply strives to satisfy hunger in order to survive and has no sense of identity; however, as experience is acquired, a part of the id eventually becomes more organized and separates. This is the ego. In Freud's less technical writings, it corresponds with the notion of 'the self'. It has a managerial function, insofar as it initiates and monitors voluntary thought and movement. If the id houses the passions, then the ego is the seat of reason. Unlike the id, which is wholly unconscious, the ego has conscious, preconscious and unconscious regions.

At a later point in infancy, the process of organization and separation occurs again. This new part of the mind is called the superego. It loosely corresponds with the notion of 'conscience' and its operation is governed by parental and societal attitudes and values. These will have been 'absorbed' by the growing child. Like the ego, the superego operates at all three levels of consciousness.

The ego occupies an extraordinarily stressful position. It must transact with the 'real world', but at the same time deal with two opposing task masters with very different objectives. The id is constantly seeking to bias voluntary action in such a

way as to satisfy libidinal urges whereas the superego is
constantly seeking to constrain voluntary action so that it does
not transgress the individual's moral 'code of conduct'. Before
initiating action of any kind, the ego must work out a
compromise that takes into account the actual situation, the
Id's instinctual urges and the superego's demand for propriety.
If libidinal urges or strict moral indictments threaten to
overwhelm the ego, the individual will experience anxiety,
guilt, or a combination of the two. Thus, an individual's mind
can exist in a state of harmony, or conflict.

These ideas have much in common with Plato's account of
the soul as described in *Phaedrus*. He suggested that the soul, or
mind, is like a chariot with two horses. One of these horses is 'of
noble stock', while the other is the exact opposite, base and
impulsive. The task of the charioteer, like the task of the ego, is
difficult and demanding. To move forward, the charioteer must
steer a course that satisfies both members of his team.

The compromise reached between the conflicting demands
of the id and superego may require the activation of a defence
mechanism. These mechanisms are initiated automatically and
the individual is unaware that they are operating. They are the
'tools' that the ego uses to negotiate a compromise between
the id and the superego. The most basic defence mechanism is
repression. If an unacceptable wish enters awareness, this may
result in anxiety. Such a wish is therefore repressed and anxiety
subsides. When repression occurs, unacceptable thoughts or
wishes are forced out of awareness into the unconscious
regions of the mind. Defence mechanisms, therefore, work in
much the same way as a central heating thermostat. When
room temperature reaches a set point, the heating system
switches itself off. When room temperature drops below that
set point, the heating system switches itself on again. Thus, the
room is kept at a comfortable temperature. When sexual
impulses become too uncomfortable, repression occurs;
however, sexual impulses do not always cause discomfort and
repression might subsequently be lifted. The operation of
defence mechanisms is routine and necessary for the
maintenance of mental equilibrium. This state of mental
equilibrium is analogous to a comfortable room temperature.

On the whole, psychologists and the interested layperson are neither offended nor perplexed by Freudian theory as it has so far been described; however, embedded within this overall framework is a theory of sexual development. It provides an account of how human beings achieve sexual maturity. For Freud's critics, the theory of sexual development is commonly held to be the weakest area of his thinking. This is probably because it is founded on a concept that many regard as either implausible or simply perverse: infant sexuality. However, Freud's use of the term sexuality in this context is in need of some clarification. When Freud refers to sexual pleasure, he can be referring to erotic pleasure, or alternatively, something much less precise. This second sense of the word 'sexual' should be interpreted as meaning 'physical' or 'satisfying'. Therefore, when Freud writes about infants deriving sexual pleasure from the erogenous zones of the body, he is not referring to an experience that is equivalent to adult sexual excitement.

Freud suggested that sexual, or at least sensual, feelings are present from birth; however, such feelings are usually forgotten by adulthood. There are two broad periods in which sexual development takes place: infancy and puberty. These are separated by a hiatus during which sexual interest diminishes, or more typically, disappears. This is called the *latency period*. Infant sexual development is more complex than puberty and is consequently broken down into three stages: the *oral phase*, the *anal phase*, and the *phallic–Oedipal phase*. Each of these phases is characterized by sexual interest becoming focused on a particular area of the body.

The first part of the body to capture 'sexual' interest is the mouth. Babies continue to suck at the nipple even after their nutritional needs have been met. Freud suggested that sucking is maintained because the newborn infant finds it pleasurable. Indeed, when the nipple is unavailable, a baby will use its thumb as a substitute. Freud argued that 'sexual' urges are therefore satisfied by oral stimulation. The oral phase is initiated at birth and ends at about one year.

Between the ages of one and three, the infant begins to derive pleasure from retaining or eliminating faeces; however, both of these come to acquire a symbolic value. The production of a stool is often welcomed by parents as something of an achievement. This provides the infant with a method for defying parental authority; namely, by retention. The period in which 'sexuality' becomes associated with bowel functioning is termed the anal phase.

The phallic–Oedipal phase of development extends from the third to the fifth or sixth years. All infants, irrespective of gender, are at first profoundly attached to their mothers. From the infant's point of view, 'mother' is the source of all nourishment, tenderness and care. 'Father', on the other hand, is a relatively remote figure; however, as the infant gets older, the father begins to assume a more prominent role. The way that boys and girls respond to an increasing awareness of the father is quite different and is influenced by a complementary growing awareness of the anatomical features that distinguish the sexes. Indeed, paraphrasing Napoleon, Freud proclaimed that 'anatomy is destiny'.

At around the age of three, boys begin to feel sexually attracted to their mothers. This coincides with a shift of sexual interest from the anus to the penis. The capacity for the genitals to provide pleasurable sensations is usually first discovered by accident, for example, when washing in the bath. It is also about this time that boys discover that girls do not have a penis. A common threat to discourage little boys from 'playing with themselves' in public is castration, for example, 'If you carry on doing that I'll cut it off!' Freud believed that awareness of the seemingly 'incomplete' female genitalia and insensitive parental reprimands combine to produce *castration anxiety*.

The Oedipal situation casts the father in the role of an angry rival, competing for the mother's affection. In the already troubled infant mind, fears develop concerning the nature of paternal retribution. The child already has some inkling that his sexual feelings towards his mother are futile; the threat of castration settles the issue and Oedipal desires are repressed. As the Oedipus complex disintegrates, the superego begins to emerge as a separate part of the child's mental architecture. The psychoanalytic historian, Peter Gay, describes the process in the following way: 'The boy's Oedipus complex is assaulted and smashed by the parental threat of castration. Then, much like a builder using stones from a demolished house, the boy incorporates broken remains of the complex into his ego and constructs his superego from them.' At this point, the period of infant sexuality ends and there is diminished interest in seeking physical pleasure.

Like boys, girls begin the phallic–Oedipal stage of development when sexual interest is transferred from the anus to the genital area. However, the young girl soon discovers that she does not have a penis. This results in a feeling of inferiority with respect to boys and the emergence of *penis envy*. She blames her mother for allowing a deficient birth, or alternatively, concludes that her mother has castrated her. Subsequently, the infant rejects her mother and begins to transfer her affection to her father (whom she now believes may be capable of giving her a penis). For the young girl, the Oedipus complex has now been replaced by the *Elektra complex*. She is attracted to her father and perceives her mother as a hostile rival.

Normal development then proceeds with the wish for a penis being gradually replaced by the wish for a baby. Although the young girl then enters the latency period, she does so in a less dramatic and less conclusive way than her male counterpart. She is, of course, free from worries about retributive castration; subsequently, 'forbidden' ideas are repressed with less vigour. Indeed, she may remain in the Elektra mode for an indeterminate length of time. In the young man, the superego is built from the debris of the demolished Oedipus complex. In the young girl, there is no such material. For her, the superego is patched together in a more ramshackle way, guided by vague fears that the expression of sexuality will result in the loss of parental love. Given these inauspicious conditions, Freud concluded that women never achieve the moral strength of men, and that women are prone to suffer from unresolved sexual feelings towards their fathers. The early experience of penis envy was also thought to equip women with a greater capacity for jealousy than men. Needless to say, these ideas have prompted lively discussion since their first espousal in the early 1920s.

Given Freud's ideas on the workings of the mind and the role of sexuality, it is now possible to summarize the process of 'normal' development. After birth, the child progresses from the oral to genital stages, becoming progressively more adult with respect to sexual preference. That is, sexual pleasure becomes strongly associated with genital stimulation. By adolescence, Oedipal issues should have been largely resolved, notwithstanding a more tenacious Elektra complex in girls. Sexual desires are satisfied by increased interest in opposite-sex peers, and fears of retribution from the same-sex parent diminish. The ego is protected from the anxiety-provoking demands of the id by the operation of defence mechanisms. These defence mechanisms are relatively modest and do not 'drain' energy that might be profitably used for other functions. A strong ego is able to procure sexual satisfaction without violating social mores. With respect to the superego, good parenting will result in the development of sensible standards of behaviour; however, minor transgressions will not evoke strong feelings of guilt. A healthy superego might be considered the source of constructive, rather than damaging, criticism.

It is a common error to confuse Freud's writings on normal development with those on *abnormal development*. For example, the Oedipus complex is often discussed as a psychological problem in itself. Yet, from his earliest writings on the subject, Freud made it quite clear that 'being in love with one and hating the other part of the parental pair' was the lot of all humanity. The Oedipus and Elektra complexes are necessary way-stations on the journey from infancy to adulthood. It is only when complexes appropriate to infancy remain influential in adulthood that problems arise.

What then were the psychological problems that Freud attempted to understand and explain? Although Freud published only five detailed case studies, he 'analysed' an extraordinary number of patients. Not surprisingly, he had something to say about most forms of mental illness; however, his most successful writings focus on the *neuroses*, a broad class of psychological problems usually associated with irrational fears. *Phobias* such as *agoraphobia* (a fear of open spaces) or *claustrophobia* (a fear of closed spaces) are the most characteristic examples of a 'neurotic illness'. Today, many of Freud's neurotic patients would be described as having an *anxiety disorder*.

When Freud began his study of fearful and anxious patients, he was undertaking a bold new venture. The standard textbooks of his day allocated only a few lines to anxiety. In retrospect, this represents a scarcely believable oversight. Anxiety disorders are now widely recognized as the most common of all psychological problems. The fact that Freud realized the importance of anxiety is clear evidence of his clinical acumen. Indeed, as early as 1895, he argued that anxiety problems were so important that they should be considered a distinct group, separate from other 'nervous conditions'. He coined the term *anxiety neurosis* to describe them, a term that gained general acceptance for most of the twentieth century. It has only recently been superseded by the term anxiety disorder.

Freud spoke of birth as 'the first great anxiety state'. All subsequent experiences of anxiety represent, at least in part, a re-creation of the sensations and feelings evoked at the time of birth. The notion that *birth trauma* could play a significant role in the subsequent development of anxiety problems was a feature of Freud's writings throughout his life; however, he never integrated the idea into the mainstream of his thinking. From the very beginning, Freud's theories about the origins of anxiety were inextricably linked with sexuality.

His early clinical observations suggested to him that anxious individuals were, for whatever reason, not releasing sexual tension. Thus, he concluded that there was an accumulation of sexual energy in the nervous system which eventually became converted into anxiety. This was a purely physical process. He compared it to wine turning into vinegar. Ultimately, Freud abandoned this idea in favour of a more 'psychological' theory of anxiety. The edifice of his revised theory was built on Oedipal foundations.

As suggested above, it is the lot of all humanity to experience Oedipal feelings. The destruction, or at least repression, of the Oedipus complex is essential for normal development. If the

Oedipus complex is not abandoned or destroyed, then this can cause problems in later life. In adulthood, the ego must wrestle with infantile wishes that have been slumbering in the id. At puberty, biological changes in the body herald the re-emergence of sexual feelings. Given that physical maturation has now made consummation of Oedipal wishes possible, sexual feelings provoke high levels of anxiety. For young women, in whom the Elektra complex is never completely resolved, adolescence is also a difficult time.

In order to reduce this anxiety, the ego protects itself by erecting defences; however, a price must be paid. If too much energy is recruited for repression, then there will less energy available for other uses and the individual's general ability to function suffers. To employ a military analogy, if the ongoing process of life is represented by an advancing army, then establishing garrisons at various stages will inevitably weaken its remaining strength. An ego weakened by too much repression is less able to deal with the demands of everyday life. Moreover, defences are rarely foolproof; subsequently, anxiety associated with forbidden desires may 'break through' if the defensive system is weakened by external factors such as stress.

Freud suggested hostile feelings towards the same-sex parent may be turned inwards. This might be experienced as self-hate or self-loathing. Such negative feelings commonly arise in depression. Thus, the survival of the Oedipus and Elektra complexes into adulthood will also provide ample scope for the development of melancholic mental states.

Freud's theory of sexual development suggests that individuals progress through oral, anal and Oedipal stages before adulthood; however, stressful experiences may cause the individual to 'get stuck' on the way. The technical term employed by Freud to describe this phenomenon is *fixation*. The earlier and more complete the fixation, the less chance the individual has of achieving sexual maturity. An individual 'fixated' at the oral stage may still seek oral gratification. Unhelpful habits such as an addiction to smoking or a compulsion to overeat may represent residual attempts at satisfying this oral need.

Even when sexual maturity is achieved, stress can still cause the individual to 'slip backward'. The technical term to describe this phenomenon is *regression*. Both fixation and regression will result in the re-emergence of infantile wishes. Clearly, the preoccupations of infancy will cause discomfort if they invade the mind of the adult, calling again for the deployment of energy-sapping defences.

The way in which the ego defends itself against the anxiety produced by infantile wishes will influence the type of symptom that emerges. One of Freud's most famous cases, known as the 'Rat Man' to preserve his anonymity, experienced excessive concern that he would cause harm to others. For example, he would iron his cash to destroy infectious bacteria which might otherwise be passed on to vulnerable recipients. Freud suggested that the Rat Man's exaggerated concern for the welfare and safety of others might be an example of a defence called *reaction formation*. When reaction formation occurs, the individual masks real feelings by intensifying their opposite. Thus, the Rat Man's concern about the safety of others was a defence against his own hostile and aggressive impulses that could be traced back to an unresolved Oedipus complex. Freud identified a number of defences. Taken together, they provide sufficient scope for understanding the full range of symptoms associated with anxiety problems.

These then are the essential components of Freud's theoretical ideas on the formation of neurotic symptoms, most notably those relating to irrational fears and worries. Notwithstanding the detail, a number of general principles can be extracted from Freud's writing on the formation of symptoms. These relate to all forms of mental illness. Firstly, symptoms are in fact the result of defences that operate to keep unacceptable material out of the conscious mind. Secondly, unacceptable thoughts and feelings have their origin in childhood experiences. Finally, all symptoms are caused by a conflict of interests between different parts of the mind. Anxiety and other distressing mental states arise from a battle waged between the higher and lower agencies of the mind.

Freud likened the process of treatment to the efforts of the Dutch to reclaim land formerly covered by the Zuider Zee. The land is like the ego, while the waters that threaten to engulf it are like the id. When an individual is suffering from a mental illness, it is as though the sea level rises and areas of land are covered over. Geographical features that should be visible simply vanish beneath the flood. Thoughts, feelings and behaviour are controlled by unconscious parts of the mind and it is almost impossible for the patient to fathom their origin and purpose. Through psychoanalysis, parts of the mind surrendered to the unconscious are won back. As Freud put it, the ego can 'appropriate fresh portions of id. Where id was, there ego shall be.'

When treatment is successful, redundant defences can be abandoned. They are no longer needed to protect the individual from anxiety aroused by unacceptable wishes and impulses. Less energy is wasted repressing unconscious material and the ego is subsequently strengthened. The ego is more independent of the superego and decisions can be made without fear of punishment or retribution. In the absence of excessive defences the individual is more in touch with reality; perception of everyday events is no longer distorted. Freud said that psychotherapy gives 'the patient's ego freedom to decide one way or another'. The individual is liberated from the constraints and influence of the past and is able to live life fully in the present.

People have always recognized that distressing thoughts and feelings may have origins that escape immediate understanding. In his *Pensées*, Pascal wrote: 'The heart has its reasons, which reason knows not.' Psychoanalysis attempts to lay bare the 'heart's reasons'. *Insight*, therefore, is one of the principal goals of psychoanalytic treatment. With the help of the analyst, the patient gains a fresh understanding of perplexing mental phenomena. To gain insight, it is essential to lift defences and retrieve lost memories.

The retrieval of significant memories from the unconscious is a difficult process. Freud's preferred method was *free association*. The patient is simply instructed to say whatever comes to mind. All critical faculties must be suspended while this is undertaken. Thus, words are spoken without any obvious purpose. In the absence of constraints, the mind is inclined to drift towards topics of significance; however, defences are still operating.

Therefore, the true meaning of the patient's words may be obscured. The analyst must interpret the patient's speech and observe the effect of the interpretation on the patient. Careful observation may reveal that a particular interpretation has special meaning. For example, the patient may become anxious or restless. Alternatively, the patient might become hostile, rejecting the interpretation as nonsense. These responses suggest that the analyst's interpretation is significant. 'A raw nerve' has been touched. Freud suggested that the most meaningful memories are the least accessible. They may be buried deep in the unconscious. In such cases, interpretations might not provoke any responses. Nevertheless, the observant analyst need not despair. The mind is always giving itself away. Minds leak information all of the time.

Although significant memories can be repressed, they are not inactive. They continue to influence speech and behaviour. Freud suggested that 'He who has eyes to see and ears to hear becomes convinced that mortals can keep no secret. If their lips are silent they gossip with their fingertips; betrayal forces its way through every pore.' He identified a particular class of betrayals, which he called the *parapraxes*. The most notable example of the parapraxes is the now famous *Freudian slip*. People often say things by mistake; however, when these errors are given careful consideration, it becomes clear that they often reveal a 'true' intention or wish. It is as if the censoring process that edits speech for the public arena suddenly fails. Thus, a guilty husband might mean to say 'I have never been unfaithful' to his wife, but instead say 'I have never been faithful'. Sometimes, such inadvertent admissions are not even noticed by the speaker. Parapraxes can also take a wide range of other forms such as the forgetting of names, words or intentions, slips of the pen, misreadings, bungled actions and mislaying things. Errors of this kind are nothing less than gaps in the patient's defensive armour, allowing the analyst to steal a glance at the patient's undiscovered self; however, for Freud, both free association and the examination of parapraxes were techniques that paled into insignificance when compared to the psychoanalyst's principal investigative tool: dream interpretation.

Freud believed that in sleep the barrier between the unconscious and conscious mind weakens. As a consequence, urges and desires usually contained in the unconscious can enter awareness; however, the conscious mind is still capable of censoring offensive material. It does so by transforming unacceptable material into images that will not disturb the sleeper. Thus, Freud distinguished between the *manifest* (or disguised) and *latent* (or undisguised) content of dreams. The disguised content is what the dreamer recalls on waking, the disjointed, sometimes bizarre images of the dream world. The undisguised content is the dream's true form. It can only be discovered by employing a specific procedure.

During psychoanalysis, the disguised content of the dream is completely ignored. Even if the dream is in the form of a relatively straightforward story, the 'narrative' is disregarded. Each element of the dream (be it an image, thought or feeling) is isolated and used as a cue for free association. In the usual way, the patient's associations will drift towards memories of significance. The analyst may see themes that link these various memories. If so, the meaning of the complete dream will become apparent. The analyst will have arrived at a full interpretation, that is, the latent or undisguised content.

The process by which unacceptable material is transformed into the disguised content of a dream was given a name by Freud: the *dream work*. The process depends on the operation of certain mechanisms, the most notable of which are *condensation, displacement* and *symbolization*. When condensation occurs, several ideas or images are conflated. Thus, a single idea can stand for many associations. Displacement is the term used to describe the separation of an 'emotion' from its causes and its subsequent attachment to other dream elements. A seemingly innocuous situation in a dream may be filled with menace that has been borrowed from elsewhere. Symbolization is the process whereby certain unacceptable objects are transformed into acceptable alternatives. For example knives, daggers and pistols may appear in the dream world as substitutes for an image of a penis.

The function of the dream work is to protect sleep, which is clearly a very necessary human activity. Ideas and feelings that would otherwise disturb sleep can enter awareness with impunity, having been suitably disguised. Sometimes, the dream work is unable to disguise unacceptable ideas and images, and the true nature of the dream begins to emerge. When this happens, the dream becomes suffused with anxiety, which may be sufficiently intense to wake the dreamer.

What then is the nature of the unacceptable material that must be censored and edited in dreams? Freud suggested that dreams provide a means of releasing tension associated with forbidden wishes. Given the importance of libido in Freud's general theory of mental life, it should come as no surprise that most of these wishes relate to sexual gratification.

The analyst also has another tool at his or her disposal: the relationship he or she cultivates with the patient. Freud sat behind his patients and adopted a neutral attitude. In fact, he recommended the surgeon's *coldness of feeling*. According to Freud, 'The physician should be opaque to the patient and, like a mirror, show nothing but what is shown to him'. This seemingly insensitive attitude has a specific purpose. The analyst becomes like a blank screen on which the patient projects elements of earlier meaningful relationships. If the psychoanalyst is neutral, then any inappropriate exchanges can be more confidently attributed to the effect of the past. For example, the Elektra complex may result in a female patient behaving in a flirtatious way towards her male analyst. This process of enacting past relationships in the present is entirely unconscious. Freud called this process *transference*. He believed it to be one of the richest sources of information about the patient. By interpreting the transference, the patient learns about the nature of past relationships, and more importantly, learns to combat their influence in the present.

It has already been noted that in 1932 Freud reflected on the fifty-year-old case of Anna O. He suggested that when Bertha Pappenheim had declared her phantom pregnancy, Breuer had 'held the key in his hand' and had chosen to drop it. With the benefit of hindsight, he was able to point out that 'the key' was the transference. When Pappenheim declared that Breuer had made her pregnant, she was revealing a wealth of information about herself. The love that she felt for Breuer was nothing less than the forbidden love she had felt for her father. In her hysterical condition, her Elektra complex had begun to influence her feelings towards Breuer in a spectacular way. Breuer had failed to interpret his relationship with his patient. He was never able, therefore, to uncover the ultimate cause of her symptoms.

In summary, the psychoanalyst attempts to treat a patient by combating self-deception. The tools of the trade are free association, careful observation of the patient, discussion of parapraxes, dream interpretation and the transference. Once the patient has gained insight, redundant defences are abandoned and the ego is strengthened. The process of psychoanalysis is similar to archaeology. Indeed, Freud told one of his patients, the 'Wolf Man', that 'the psychoanalyst, like the archaeologist in his excavations, must uncover layer after layer of the patient's psyche, before coming to the deepest, most valuable treasures.' Such excavations take time, and Freud expected analysis to take several years. Indeed, he saw most patients six times a week in order to ensure continuity. To enter traditional Freudian analysis is far more like adopting a new way of life than undertaking a course of treatment. Clearly, Freud did not take the exhumation of the soul's dark treasures lightly.

The fact that Sir Isaac Newton was a scowling misanthrope, became paranoid in later life, and died a virgin has no implication whatsoever for Newtonian physics. The laws of motion would have been the very same laws of motion had he been an easygoing socialite with a keen interest in women. It is difficult to come to the same conclusions with respect to Freud and his theories about the mind. Although he sought to uncover universal principles, he gave particular significance to features of mental life that were of personal relevance. As such, 'Freudian psychology' was profoundly influenced by Freud's personal psychology. The two are intimately related.

It is difficult to imagine how Freud could have developed his ideas if he were anything but the staunchest of atheists. Apart from a brief flirtation with spiritual ideas in his youth, he saw religion as nothing more than a collective neurotic illness. Copernicus took the earth from the centre of the universe and

Darwin invited humanity to acknowledge its animal heritage. Freud described his work as the third and 'most wounding blow' to 'human megalomania'. Given the importance of unconscious processes, we are barely aware of ourselves. Such an account of humanity could only be endorsed by an individual who was a complete stranger to religious faith.

Freud was obsessed with the classical world. Indeed, Freud's consulting room was full of antiquities. One of his patients, recalling his analysis, said that Freud's room was nothing like a doctor's practice. Instead, it looked like the study of an archaeologist. It was littered with statues and icons, engravings and artefacts. Indeed, Freud once claimed to have read more archaeology than psychology. The idea that the mind could be excavated was clearly influenced by his consuming passion for the classical world.

On Freud's fiftieth birthday, his admirers presented him with a medallion. On one side was his profile; on the other, Oedipus solving the riddle of the sphinx. The inscription, which was taken from Sophocles, read: 'He divined the famous riddle and was a most mighty man.' For Freud, the mind was like the sphinx, concealing and withholding secrets. He, Sigmund Freud, had developed a method that could reveal the nature of those secrets. The comparison between Oedipus and himself was a particularly meaningful one for Freud. He was of course deeply attracted to his mother; however, the links between the story of Oedipus and his life became even more significant over time.

The concept of the Elektra complex, if not inspired by his relationship with his daughters, was certainly consolidated by a close attachment to Anna, the youngest of his daughters. Freud discouraged her prospective suitors and seemed intent on keeping her for himself. Moreover, these feelings were reciprocated. In 1915, Anna wrote to her father: 'Recently I dreamt that you are a king and I a princess, that people want to separate us . . .'

In later life he called her his 'Antigone'. In *Oedipus at Colonus*, the blind, aging king is guided and cared for by his doting daughter. This too was Anna's destiny. When Freud became elderly and infirm, she was his constant companion. By his own admission, she had become more important to him than his wife, and their relationship was so close that he (the most committed of all sceptics) believed that they could communicate by telepathy! Anna Freud never married. Freud's colleagues, sensitive to the implications of the Elektra complex, believed that no suitor could ever compete with the great love of her life. The old man was, after all, an extremely difficult act to follow.

Freud became the foremost authority on neurotic illnesses, especially anxiety disorders. During the course of his life, he suffered from a range of irrational fears. When courting his future wife, he became pathologically jealous. He was unhappy about the affectionate bonds that she shared with her immediate family, and even insisted that she should be less familiar with her cousins. For no good reason, he was terrified that he would lose her. For years he harboured the belief that he would die at the age of 51. This belief was later exchanged for the belief that he would die at 61 or 62. He became particularly worried when he was assigned a telephone number that ended with the digits 6 and 2, considering it to be an omen. Needless to say, his concern was unfounded. He lived to the age of 83. The most extraordinary of his irrational fears was a phobic avoidance of Rome. He was desperate to visit the city, but when he got to Lake Trasimeno, about a hundred miles north of Rome, he had to inexplicably turn back. He eventually overcame this mental block and suffered no ill consequences. It would seem that he could empathize with his patients because he was so accustomed to experiencing irrational fears.

One of the principal goals of psychoanalysis is to resolve internal conflicts. The human mind is a battleground, on which an internecine war is ceaselessly waged between primitive desires and noble aspirations. Man is a creature of contradictions. Freud was a man whose life and writings are full of contradictions. He believed that the brain and nervous system were the ultimate cause of mental illness. Indeed, he proposed with some relish that, one day, drugs might be developed that could alter the brain and therefore make his life's work entirely redundant. Yet he developed a purely psychological treatment for healing the mind. He sought to discover the universal principles that governed behaviour, yet based his theories on his own personal experience and self-analysis. He was proud of being a Jew, yet he published a critical work on Judaism at a time when thousands of Jews were being transported to concentration camps. He claimed that the discovery of truth was his single and most valued aim, but when he met Einstein in 1930, he said: 'I no longer count as one of my merits that I always tell the truth'. At the end of a life in which posterity was never far from his thoughts, he destroyed most of his personal papers to deter biographers. It is no surprise, given the above, that a man full of contradictions should give internal conflict a central position in human suffering.

Even the most elusive of Freud's ideas can be better understood in the context of his personal psychology, for example, his concept of the death instinct. At first sight, this concept does not seem to make much sense. Indeed, many of his devotees found it entirely implausible. It is often suggested that Freud's concept of the death instinct was introduced after he had witnessed the horrors of the First World War; however, the man and the idea share a far more intimate relationship on closer examination.

In 1923, Freud was told that he had developed cancer of the mouth. He was advised to stop smoking, but simply refused to. Towards the end of his life, his mouth was rotting to the extent that his pet dog was distressed by the smell and parts had been replaced by a prosthesis. He continued to smoke, ignoring his physician's advice. At times, he openly wished for death. He even wrote that if his illness killed him it 'would be very desirable'. Of course, his wish to end it all was very much influenced by his intolerable pain and suffering; however, he viewed the prospect of death with curious equanimity.

On 21 September 1939, he reminded his physician that they had once agreed a 'contract'. His physician could hardly have forgotten. Freud thanked him for remembering and asked him to consult Anna before going ahead; however, it was very clear what he hoped the decision would be. Soon after, the physician administered a lethal dose of morphine. Before sunrise on 23 September, Freud was dead. It is said that he died with dignity

and without a trace of self-pity. Like almost all of his ideas, the
death instinct was not an academic abstraction, but a personal
reality.

CHAPTER 3

After Freud

"'Tis not the great disproportion betwixt ourself and another,
which produces envy; but on the contrary, our proximity.'
David Hume, *A Treatise of Human Nature*

As a child, Freud identified strongly with the Carthaginian
general, Hannibal – the Semite, who had dared to do battle
with the might of Rome. So inspiring was Hannibal to the
young Freud that for some time he thought that he might
pursue a military career. From the very beginning then, his
personality was inclined towards conquests and the building of
an empire. Although his talents as a strategist were never
utilized by the Austro-Hungarian army, they proved
indispensable as the Vienna Psychoanalytic Society began to
grow. Unfortunately, the process of conquest and expansion
was fraught with difficulties. Freud often blamed delays and
setbacks on the medical establishment and bourgeois prudery;
however, the most significant obstacles to advancement came,
not from the staunch advocates of conservatism, but rather
from his closest allies. Even as the first battles and skirmishes
were being won under the banner of psychoanalysis, Freud's
troops were turning against him. His followers were always
eager to turn a theoretical difference into a crisis. The fact that
the psychoanalytic movement survived at all is quite
remarkable, for no sooner had one dissenting group been
appeased or silenced than another would appear. With the
exception of his 'Antigone', no one proved entirely worthy of
his trust. Steering the psychoanalytic movement into the
twentieth century was a task requiring guile, diplomacy and
tact.

Any new movement is destined to evolve in a climate of diverging opinion and lively debate. Even though a general framework of ideas may already exist, there will still be considerable scope for argument. This is usually because the detail of the framework has yet to be worked out. The process of debate is a group endeavour, which, through compromise, separates the grain from the chaff. Poor ideas are abandoned, while good ideas are retained. As a result of this procedure, the movement becomes stronger as a whole.

In the early years of the psychoanalytic movement, differences of opinion were only rarely resolved through compromise. Once a rift appeared, it tended only to widen. These 'early schismatics', as they are sometimes called, included names such as Otto Rank, Wilhelm Stekel, Sándor Ferenczi and Wilhelm Reich; however, Alfred Adler and Carl Gustav Jung remain the most well-known of those who broke with Freud before the 1920s. Contemplating this group of dissidents, the psychiatrist J. A. C. Brown writes: 'One is led to believe that Freud . . . was surrounded by a group of egocentric primadonnas whose highly ambivalent devotion to the Master was only equalled by their dislike of each other.' Ironically, Freud's querulous followers seemed intent on re-enacting the Oedipal drama with which they often took issue. Freud, cast in the role of the father, became the recipient of their hostility. In the same way that the infant son wishes to dispose of his father so that he might take his place, so it was that the most talented of Freud's disciples wished to dispose of Freud in order to occupy his seat at the head of the table.

Notwithstanding the shortcomings of his disciples, some of the blame for the fragmentation of the Freudian empire must rest with Freud himself. Throughout his life he established intense friendships with colleagues who inspired him to develop and refine his ideas. Unfortunately, these friendships usually ended badly. The intimacy that Freud encouraged was clearly inappropriate within the context of a professional relationship. Eventually, technical differences and personal differences became hopelessly confused. Had Freud shown more restraint in his role as a friend, he may well have suffered less in his role as a teacher.

In retrospect, it would seem that the early schismatics established something of a precedent. Since 1911, major analysts who have entertained ideas that diverge from Freudian orthodoxy have, on the whole, favoured the radical solution of founding a new 'school', rather than choosing to resolve differences within the psychoanalytic establishment. Although there are certain very basic ideas that link all of these diverse schools, psychoanalysis has not progressed by consensus. This would suggest that the initial wounds inflicted by the early schismatics have never truly healed.

The first, and some would argue the deepest, wound sustained by the psychoanalytic establishment was inflicted by a man who occupied a prestigious position in the burgeoning Vienna Psychoanalytic Society. Indeed, among the luminaries that made up the membership of the Wednesday Club, Alfred Adler was considered an intellect second only to Freud himself. Reports of his character are mixed. On the one hand, some observers described him as sulky and eager for recognition, whereas others praised his relaxed attitude and good humour. There can be little doubt that, at least initially, Freud's attitude to Adler was positive. He welcomed the younger man's contributions and looked upon his work as complementary to his own; however, this cordiality was never really reciprocated. Unlike the other members of Freud's inner circle, Adler was never happy in the role of pupil or disciple. He regarded himself instead as a junior colleague, an independent thinker with a distinctive voice and approach. From the very beginning, his writings bear the impression of an Adlerian stamp.

Initially, Adler was attracted to psychoanalysis because of its biological foundations; however, he was to become increasingly interested in a particular biological mechanism called *compensation*. When a specific organ is weak, the body often adapts itself so that the deficiency is remedied. It would seem that the body is able to overcome some of its less serious defects through self-regulation. Adler suggested that the mind operates in a similar way. For example, individuals with a mild speech problem might compensate and eventually become great orators. Winston Churchill is a typical example of this kind of person. Adler elaborated these ideas in a work published in 1907 called *A Study of Organic Inferiority and Its Psychical Compensation.* Freud did not object to Adler's observations. Indeed, he was very interested in his work; however, it soon became apparent that Adler was not merely seeking to enrich psychoanalysis, but rather to lay the foundations of an alternative mental science – a system of understanding the mind which he called *individual psychology.*

By 1910, Freud had become deeply concerned about Adler; even so, his correspondence suggests frustration rather than anger: 'He is always . . . forcing me into the unwelcome role of the aging despot who prevents young men from getting ahead,' wrote Freud to a colleague. Unfortunately, their relationship became more and more strained as Adler openly challenged the basic tenets of psychoanalysis. He disputed the importance of unconscious sexual ideas and then went on to reject infant sexuality, the Oedipus complex, and the sexual origins of anxiety. At this time, Freud did not consider Adler an intellectual threat; however, he was nevertheless worried for political reasons. He feared that Adler was developing a sanitized version of psychoanalysis that would be more acceptable to both the medical establishment and the general public.

Adler's individual psychology lacks much of the tortuous complexity of traditional Freudian psychoanalysis; however, its strengths are at the same time its weaknesses. Adler's beliefs about normal development, the origins of mental illness and the role of compensation are refreshingly straightforward, but very much open to the charge of oversimplification.

According to Adler, all children naturally feel small and helpless. Therefore, they must develop strategies that help them to compensate for these feelings of inferiority. The set of attitudes that the growing individual develops to conquer feelings of inferiority Adler called the *life style.* It is these same attitudes that become a template for the adult personality.

The selection of compensatory coping strategies is largely determined by constitution, gender and circumstances. Therefore, an anxious girl who is also the first born in a family, will select different strategies to compensate for feelings of inferiority than a more robust younger brother. The strategies that are found to be the most effective in childhood tend to be those that are retained in adulthood.

In Freudian psychoanalysis, maturation is intimately linked with sexuality. For Adler, the principal issues are not sexual but social. Maturation is all about striving for power, prestige and superiority. Growing up requires the selection of strategies that best compensate for the initial position of disadvantage shared by all children. There are three possible outcomes associated with striving for superiority.

The first of these is *successful compensation*. The individual adjusts to his or her deficiencies in an appropriate way and suffers no ill consequences. Adler's second outcome is *Overcompensation*. Here, compensation is extreme and the response to an early deficiency results in the development of an exaggerated 'opposite tendency'. For example, a weakling who suffers at the hands of bullies at school might become a gangster in later life. The third outcome that Adler described was *Retreat into illness*. According to Adler, becoming 'mentally ill' allows the individual to avoid situations that will heighten awareness of feelings of inferiority. Thus, the illness has a function. It provides an excuse, usually accepted by society, for being unable to meet the sometimes difficult challenges of growing and developing as a person. The 'illness' might also be used as a kind of tool to manipulate or gain control over others such as in emotional blackmail. To be mentally ill, therefore, is a type of solution, an unhelpful way of adjusting to life's complexities.

Adlerian psychotherapy is considerably more straight-forward than traditional psychoanalysis. The inscrutable remoteness of the Freudian analyst is dispensed with in favour of a more natural kind of relationship. The therapist is permitted to empathize and problems are discussed in much the same way as an everyday conversation. Dream interpretation is retained, but only insofar as the dream is thought to represent a struggle with a contemporary problem. Moreover, Adler rejected Freud's detailed analysis of the content of dreams and suggested that it was more important to examine the dream's emotional tone. After analysing a problem, in terms of a poor adjustment to feelings of inferiority, the therapist suggests new ways of coping. Less helpful strategies must be replaced by more helpful strategies. Realistic goals are set and the patient is urged to modify both attitudes and behaviour. The whole process requires considerably fewer sessions than traditional psychoanalysis.

On the verge of Adler's secession, Freud asked him not to leave the psychoanalytic movement. Adler's reply was succinct and meaningful: 'Why should I always do my work under your shadow?' Late in February 1911, Adler resigned as presiding officer of the Vienna Psychoanalytic Society. Thereafter, the only thing shared by the two men was mutual loathing. So much so that 26 years later, when Freud learned of Adler's death, he expressed only satisfaction.

Adler was a deeply committed socialist. Ironically, the idea of the individual *striving for power* struck a sympathetic chord in America, where competitive capitalism has always been championed. He was a major influence on American schools of psychotherapy, most notably a group known as the Neo-Freudians, which included several distinguished native and émigré analysts. Erich Fromm, Karen Horney and Harry Stack Sullivan are perhaps the most widely read of this group. As a result of Adler's influence, psychoanalysis was forced to pay greater attention to the ego and the conscious mind. This aspect of his influence extended far beyond the Neo-Freudian school.

If the relationship between Alfred Adler and Sigmund Freud was never close, then its antithesis could be found in the early relationship between Freud and Carl Gustav Jung. Of all Freud's followers, it was Jung who basked most in the great man's favour. Freud called him his 'Crown Prince'. Jung had none of the superficial characteristics that might distinguish him as the heir apparent. He was neither Viennese nor, more importantly, Jewish. With respect to the latter, Freud had noted the peculiar affinity that many Jewish practitioners enjoyed with respect to his methods. His support for an individual whom he chose to describe as 'the Teuton' was unexpected.

Jung was the son of a Swiss pastor. After completing his medical training he became an assistant physician at the Burghölzli Mental Hospital in Zurich. In 1906, he sent a

volume of his work entitled *Diagnostic Association Studies* to
Freud. These studies had been undertaken by Jung and his
senior, Eugen Bleuler (the psychiatrist who invented the term
schizophrenia). Freud's ideas were copiously cited in the text,
and it was this initial contact that began a regular
correspondence that would last for seven years and eventually
acquire the status of literature.

The letters that Freud and Jung wrote to each other are quite
extraordinary. At times, they read much more like love letters
than the learned exchange of ideas between two men of
science. For example, in 1908 Freud wrote: 'I am quite certain
that after having moved a few steps away from me you will find
your way back, and then go far with me. I can't give you any
reason for this certainty; it probably springs from a feeling I
have when I look at you. But I am satisfied to feel at one with
you and no longer fear that we might be torn apart.' Some
months earlier Jung had written to Freud to confess that,
although he recognized it as both 'disgusting' and 'ridiculous',
he had an undeniable 'crush' on him! Like all great love affairs,
tragedy was inevitable.

In October 1911, Jung's wife, Emma, took the liberty of
writing a private letter to Freud. In it, she wrote: 'I have been
tormented by the idea that your relation with my husband is
not altogether as it should be . . .' Freud wrote a reassuring
letter back, but Emma had detected the hairline fractures that
presaged a shattered friendship. By the following year, Jung's
'crush' on Freud had turned into bitter resentment: 'stop
playing the father to your sons and instead of aiming
continually at their weak spots . . . [take] . . . a good look at
your own for a change . . .' After having addressed Jung not
only as his 'Crown Prince', but also as his 'Alexander', his
'Joshua' and his 'dear friend and heir', Freud began his final
letter 'Dear Doctor'. He could not even bear to write Jung's
name. What went wrong?

Like Breuer and Adler before him, Jung rejected the
overwhelming importance that Freud gave to sexuality in
mental life; however, it is clear that this theoretical difference
simply served as a convenient means of channelling his
growing frustration at being Freud's acolyte. Also, Jung

declared a penchant for all things mystical that Freud found unacceptable. At first, Freud tolerated Jung's forays into the worlds of astrology and the paranormal; nevertheless, it is clear from their correspondence that he was never entirely comfortable with his protégé's behaviour. Choosing the analogy of an exotic climate, he urged Jung not to stay in the 'tropics' for too long. Unfortunately, Jung developed a taste for the exotic that eventually permeated all his writings. His collected works seem more like a metaphysical system of beliefs than a scientific school of psychology. Indeed, J. A. C. Brown writes that one 'gets much the same impression from reading Jung as might be obtained from reading the scriptures of the Hindus, Taoists, or Confucians'.

In spite of the outlandish nature of much of Jung's writing, it is clear that he, more than any other post-Freudian, developed a framework within which to understand the mind that matches Freud's in its complexity. He called this framework *analytical psychology*. Jung is also, without doubt, the only psychotherapist to have achieved a level of cultural recognition comparable to Freud's. The 'Crown Prince' never inherited the empire as Freud had intended. Instead, he established his own.

Jung began his clinical career steeped in Freudian psychology; however, even in his first major case study, it is possible to discern themes that were to be characteristic of later work. His medical degree dissertation was entitled *On the Psychology and Pathology of So-called Occult Phenomena*. It is based on observations of his 15-year-old cousin who claimed to be a medium. During seances, the girl came under the control of various 'personalities' which Jung suggested were, in fact, *personifications* of parts of her unconscious mind. The idea that areas of the unconscious could, as it were, separate from the rest of the mind and assume a kind of independent identity became an axiom of analytical psychology. From his dissertation onwards, Jung continued to think of an individual's character as a conglomerate of *sub-personalities*.

According to Jung, mental illness arises when sub-personalities fail to act in concert. Mental health is the natural consequence of unity among the separate agencies of the mind. Freud had introduced the idea of conflict between the separate mental agencies of ego, superego and id. In Jung's scheme, the possibilities for conflict become virtually infinite as the mind is divided not by three, but into a multiplicity of separate selves.

A notion related to sub-personality that became very influential within the psychoanalytic movement as a whole was that of the *complex*. Although the two most famous complexes are Freudian, those being the Oedipus and Elektra, the term complex was first coined by Jung. However, when Jung uses the term, he is not simply referring to an unconscious group of related ideas and impulses. Rather he is referring to an elaborate network of thoughts, memories and feelings, which are so well organized that they could almost pass as an autonomous individual. A Jungian complex is not a fully fledged sub-personality, but it is very close to it.

Jung, like Freud, believed that mental life proceeds at three levels of awareness; although the *conscious* mind is retained, the unconscious mind undergoes some modification and an entirely new third domain is added. Jung described the unconscious mind as the *personal unconscious*. It contains repressed ideas and memories, as Freud suggested; however, in addition to these it also contains material that has simply been neglected. Like possessions stored in the basement for so long that they are forgotten, the personal unconscious harbours obsolete memories and feelings. Below the personal unconscious is Jung's third domain, the *collective unconscious*, a subterranean museum containing the most fundamental and shared elements of human nature and experience.

A common image used to capture how these regions of the mind relate to each other is the archipelago. Minds are likened to a chain of islands. The islands themselves are the conscious minds of individuals, and each of these has an individual structure below the water, that is, the personal unconscious; however, at a deeper level, the rock formations begin to join. The level at which a particular 'family' of islands share a common bed is equivalent to the *racial unconscious*. This is a repository of the memories of a particular racial group (for example, Mongolian or Aryan). Although Jung wrote extensively about this level of consciousness, it is now usually subsumed under the heading of the collective unconscious. Returning to the archipelago metaphor, the collective unconscious is the deepest level at which all islands are joined, that is, the seabed.

Jung inferred the existence of the collective unconscious after making certain clinical observations that struck him as uncanny. He analysed the delusions and hallucinations of patients suffering from severe mental problems such as schizophrenia, and found that they included material drawn from ancient religion and myth. The individual patients had not had access to documents that made reference to such material, yet many symbols and images were recreated in some detail during hallucinatory episodes. Jung posited a common source, which he described as 'a myth-producing level of mind which was common to all men.' Further, he suggested that the collective unconscious might also contain primitive impressions, the origins of which might be the experiences of the primate and animal ancestry of mankind.

Within the collective unconscious can be found mythological motifs or primordial images, which Jung called *Archetypes*. They are never conscious as such, but they influence and organize images and ideas in the conscious mind. The influence of the archetypes is usually 'felt' as being spiritually significant.

The concept of the archetypes is far from clear. Like Freud, Jung was also guilty of generating explanatory ideas that do not fare well under close scrutiny. Jung writes that the presence of archetypes can only be explained 'by assuming them to be deposits of the constantly repeated experiences of humanity'. He gives as an example the apparent movement of the sun. Daily experience of the sun's trajectory, disappearance and return has given rise to countless *sun-hero myths.* Jung suggested: 'The archetype is a kind of readiness to produce over and over again the same or similar mythical ideas.' It is interesting to note that Freud's self-analysis, requiring descent into and return from his own unconscious, has acquired the status of a sun-hero myth in the context of psychoanalytic folklore.

The sun-hero archetype is a particularly abstract example of the concept. It represents the theme of death and rebirth;

however, other archetypes lend themselves more readily to personification. They can be thought of as figures or people. In the same way that the sun-hero archetype might influence the stories and images of art and literature, the personified archetypes exert a particularly strong influence on the ego. When discussing the origins of psychological problems, Jung gave special emphasis to three personified archetypes: the *shadow*, the *anima* and the *animus*.

The shadow is usually the first archetype to be encountered in psychotherapy. It organizes an individual's repressed and unacceptable tendencies. These form a kind of sub-personality that might be viewed as a lesser self, childish and instinctive. There is much of the shadow that corresponds with Freud's id. The character of the shadow can be discovered by careful examination of the contents of the personal unconscious, as revealed in analysis; however, the shadow may also manifest itself more directly in everyday life. When overcome with rage, it is not uncommon for people to say: 'I wasn't myself.' It is as though the individual exchanges Dr Jekyll for Mr Hyde. The shadow is also a frequent protagonist in dreams, appearing as a primitive, proto-human or unpleasant figure that arouses dislike. Sometimes the shadow will appear in the guise of a demonic figure such as the devil.

Jung believed that the unconscious of every man conceals a complementary feminine character, while the unconscious of every woman conceals a complementary masculine character. These sub-personalities are organized by the two archetypes that he called the anima and the animus. They influence how the individual perceives members of the opposite sex and how traits usually associated with one or other gender are expressed. In men, the influence of the anima is likely to become more pronounced in situations where reason and common sense are of little use. In these situations, female characteristics such as emotional sensitivity and intuition become more apparent. In women, the influence of the animus is evident in situations requiring the exercise of logic, a mental capacity Jung associated with masculinity. Unfortunately, these complementary resources do not always work in the individual's interests. A man might become excessively moody or submissive, while a woman might become remote and aggressive. Both the anima and the animus can appear in dreams, often assuming idealized forms. Examples are *earth mother* or *warrior*.

The shadow, anima and animus may all influence behaviour in social situations according to their respective properties; however, the broad regularities that constitute an individual's social self are determined by a particular archetype, the *persona*. Jung borrowed this term from the world of classical drama, it being the mask worn by an actor to emphasize his 'character'. The persona helps us to orchestrate our social performance and corresponds very closely with the concept of 'role'. Although each persona is unique, the archetype has a collective or wider cultural dimension. When an individual constructs his or her mask, the final product may be an aggregate of impressions. For example, a creative artist may grow his hair long and adopt a very casual mode of dress, a *Bohemian* image that has gained particular currency since the nineteenth century. Such an individual is merely adopting a uniform that communicates to others knowledge of the 'group' with which he most strongly identifies. Unfortunately, this process of identification can go too far. When an individual becomes lost in his or her social role, other aspects of the personality remain undeveloped. An individual may also suffer psychologically if there is a large discrepancy between the persona he or she has chosen and the individual's 'true self', in much the same way as a comic actor, inappropriately cast as a tragic hero, would be likely to experience difficulty with the role.

The archetypes described here are merely a representative sample. There are many more, far too numerous to describe in detail. Clearly, analytical psychology with its 'myth-producing level of mind' and primordial images is highly complex. Yet this complexity is not always reflected in Jung's ideas about mental illness. In some ways, Jung's views on the origins of mental illness are more straightforward than Freud's. He believed that neurotic illness was caused by *contemporary events*, rather than those associated with infancy and early childhood. When an individual encounters misfortune, stress or failure, he or she withdraws from the outside world and turns inwards. When this happens, Oedipal needs and wishes are reactivated. The individual, in effect, experiences a regression to an earlier stage of development. Although Jung was happy to acknowledge the importance of the Oedipus complex, he did not believe Oedipal themes to be at the root of neurotic illness. The Oedipus complex was considered not a cause, but a symptom.

The Freudian notion of conflict is retained in Jung's account of psychological problems; however, the context in which conflict occurs is somewhat different. In Jung's scheme, neurotic illness arises when there is conflict between different aspects of the personality that have not developed equally. The mind is out of kilter, becoming quite literally unbalanced. Psychotherapy represents an attempt to redress this balance. Parts of the personality previously neglected are strengthened, the result of which is a synthesis of equal parts. Thus, the cold rationalist might find his or her warmer, intuitive self and vice versa. Such ideas have their modern counterpart in the axiom of counsellors that it is a good thing to 'get in touch with one's feelings' or rediscover 'the inner child'.

If Jung's collected works are compared with those of Freud, it is clear that both men were interested in quite different stages of life. Although Freud saw adult patients, his real interest was childhood. He was fascinated by the processes that give authenticity to the poet William Wordsworth's observation: 'The Child is father of the Man.' Jung, on the other hand, was far more interested in adulthood, and in particular the middle years. Analytical psychology is concerned with destiny rather than history. Nowhere is this forward-looking quality of Jung's writing more clear than when he writes about *individuation*, the journey towards wholeness that spans a lifetime and that is, in essence, a spiritual journey. The person who has undergone this process is able to integrate the diverse elements of personality and face the final challenges of life with calm acceptance and detachment. One of the principal goals of therapy is to facilitate this process.

Like Adler, Jung was a less remote figure than Freud during consultations. He urged the cultivation of an open and accepting relationship between therapist and patient; however, as in Freudian analysis, the relationship itself was thought to be a useful 'tool'. Subsequently, in Jungian analysis, the patient's feelings toward his or her therapist are often selected as a topic for discussion. Dream analysis is also retained, although the images and events in the dream are thought to reflect a neglected or underdeveloped aspect of an individual's personality. During sleep, overlooked talents and un-acknowledged feelings are free to rise from the darker regions of the mind into awareness. In the world of dreams, the soldier may become a doctor, and the doctor an executioner. Where dream interpretation reveals a vast discrepancy between waking and sleeping identities, therapy will attempt to narrow the gap, pursuing the formation of a more integrated personality.

Perhaps Jung's greatest contribution to the practice of psychotherapy was his realization that the unconscious mind might be a poor orator, but an excellent artist. What is inexpressible in words might still be communicated in an image. Jung was the first analyst to encourage patients to draw, paint and use other creative methods of self-expression. These images might then be interpreted using much the same methods as would be used in dream analysis. This particular idea has been extremely influential, and the approach to treatment now known as *art therapy* has grown in its wake. Moreover, approaches to treatment such as *music therapy* (in which patients compose and perform) and *psychodrama* (in which patients act out roles and scenarios) represent a variation on the same idea.

In addition to Jung's work on clinical problems and the practice of psychotherapy, he published numerous articles and papers of a more general nature. His description of two basic personality types, that of *introvert* and *extravert*, has been highly influential. The former type tends to be shy, inward-looking and cautious, whereas the latter tends to be outgoing, sociable and optimistic.

Jung started his career as the most scientific member of Freud's coterie. More than any other disciple, he was committed to proving the validity of psychoanalytic ideas by conducting studies and experiments. It is, therefore, a great irony that by the end of his life Jung had undergone a profound transformation. The scientist had vanished and his place was now occupied by a 'holy man'. Jung's interest in mysticism and the arcane led him to reflect on subjects as diverse as alchemy, mandalas and Tibetan Buddhism. He came to believe that the archetypes existed outside space and time and that they exerted their influence on man from a non-physical domain. Moreover, Jung suggested that it was the archetypes that were ultimately responsible for a phenomena he described as *synchronicity*, the occurrence of meaningful coincidences (for example, dreams that correspond with events happening in the real world). In 1958, he wrote on the significance of UFOs, which he considered to be omens of change in the collective mind of mankind. Even Freud, who had exhorted his young colleague not to dally in exotic climes, would have been hard pushed to guess at exactly how far from medicine Jung would wander.

Yet it is Jung's esotericism that appears to have ensured him a position of enormous cultural importance. He is a foil to Freud's materialist 'straight man'. Jung offers the spiritually bankrupt denizens of the western world a vision of the mind that is influenced by 'higher' things. He offers the patient a form of therapy in which sub-personalities and archetypes, in the guise of Wagnerian heroes, struggle to resolve inner conflicts. Jung is, for want of a better description, nothing if not entertaining. Perhaps it is for this reason that he appears to hold a special place in the affections of the artistic community. Moreover, for those without a scientific background, Jung appears to lend some legitimacy to ideas that are usually the province of mystics, psychics and theologians, although it is a legitimacy that is, without doubt, almost wholly misplaced.

In spite of Jung's broad, popular appeal, and despite the complexity and far-reaching nature of his thinking, his influence on mainstream psychology has been negligible. There are no post-Jungians. Analytical psychology, regardless of its origin in Freudian theory, is almost entirely self-contained. He has no intellectual heirs. Although the 'Crown Prince' established his own empire, it is one that few care to visit in earnest.

Under the influence of mostly Adlerian ideas, the early schismatics emphasized two fundamental shifts in the practice and theory of psychotherapy. Firstly, attempts were made to shorten the length of analysis, which was viewed as impractically long in its traditional form. Secondly, and more importantly, greater emphasis was given to the role of the ego and conscious mind than the unconscious mind and the id. This latter break with orthodoxy was encouraged, even by Freud's own daughter, Anna, in works such as *The Ego and the Mechanisms of Defence*.

Anna Freud's main contribution to her father's discipline was in the field of child analysis; however, it was another analyst specializing in the treatment of children who ultimately proved to be more influential. This was Melanie Klein. The fact that Klein's writings survived to inspire a generation of psychotherapists is interesting, insofar as she was definitely struggling against the tide of opinion. While the general trend was towards a greater appreciation of the conscious mind, Klein was exceptional in that she took the violent and aggressive world of the id even more seriously than Freud.

For a time, there was considerable debate in the psychoanalytic movement concerning the relative merits of ideas espoused by either Anna Freud or Melanie Klein. The Master tried to remain neutral, but finally expressed a clear preference for his daughter's work. Freud's deep affection for Anna must have clouded his judgement, because Klein's work is so similar in spirit to his own. Moreover, of the new generation of analysts who reached maturity in the 1920s, Klein was by far the most innovative. This would not, indeed could not, have escaped Freud's notice.

Melanie Klein was born in Vienna in 1882; however, it was only when she moved to Budapest at the age of 28 that she discovered the works of Freud. She consumed much of the psychoanalytic literature with great enthusiasm and subsequently entered analysis with one Freud's closest disciples. After training, Klein chose to specialize in the treatment of very young children. With characteristic zeal, she recruited her own children as patients and went on to write clinical papers on their development!

In 1926, Klein moved to England, where she became a highly influential figure in British psychoanalysis. Indeed, it might be said that her presence influenced the whole course of British psychoanalysis from the 1920s to the present day. Those members of the British psychoanalytic movement who proved the most responsive to Klein's ideas were eventually united under the banner of the object relations school. The term *object relations* made its first appearance in a paper published by Karl Abraham in 1924; however, it now has stronger associations with British luminaries such as Ronald Fairburn and Donald Winnicott. The basic tenet of the object relations school is that the primary motivational drive is *social*, that is, to form relationships with others. Needless to say, the first and most important relationship is established between mother and child.

Largely because of Jung, several analysts had questioned the Freudian view that the origins of mental illness could be traced back to one or two critical years occurring in early childhood. There was a growing acceptance that psychological difficulties might be attributed to a range of influences, particularly contemporary experiences and events. In spite of this trend, Klein adopted a completely different view. She believed that the origins of mental illness were even more historically remote than Freud had suggested and that the psychological fate of the individual is sealed before the first year of life comes to an end.

According to Klein, the neonate (or newborn child) is not equipped to deal with the complexities of experience. Everything must be simplified. The world is thus divided into good and bad 'objects'. In the neonate's mind, everything can be accommodated within this black and white dichotomy. There are no grey areas. The first object to acquire substantial significance in the neonate's world is its source of nutrition, the breast. Sometimes the breast will provide a plentiful supply of milk, whereas at other times the breast will be empty. These two different states will evoke in the child two corresponding emotional responses: either feelings of love and satisfaction, or feelings of anger and uncontrollable rage. There is no middle ground. The breast is either good or bad. The emotions evoked in the neonate by the plentiful and empty breasts are clearly close relatives of Eros and Thanatos, the fundamental Freudian instincts; however, whereas Freud always favoured the influence of the former in mental life, Klein favoured the latter. In the Kleinian universe, humans are shaped more in anger than by love.

The first six months of life are characterized by fear and suspicion of the bad breast. Klein called this mental state the *paranoid-schizoid position*. In the second six months of life, the infant achieves a sufficient level of intellectual sophistication to recognize that the loved and hated breast are not different entities, but the same. This recognition is accompanied by feelings of sadness, guilt and regret. Klein called this mental state the *depressive position*.

Perhaps the first major challenge in life is to work through the depressive position. The infant must learn that love is constant, in spite of all the previous rages and aggressive fantasies. Until the infant learns that love is constant, he or she will interpret all frustrations and separations as a form of retribution because of past destructive fantasies. It is essential that a good relationship is established between mother and child. The infant will not be able to develop beyond the depressive position until he or she is assured of the consistency of maternal love. Moreover, a certain amount of contrition is required. The infant must accept responsibility for destructive fantasies and experience emotions that reflect mental acts of reparation such as sorrow. Klein suggested that those infants who were unable to negotiate the depressive position would never establish a stable *internal image* of a loving object, that is, a memory of a good and healthy relationship with their mother. The absence of such a memory leaves the individual prone to depression and a range of other psychological problems.

It should be stressed that Klein gives priority to subjective experience over real events. In other words, it is the mental impression of the relationship formed between mother and child (in the child's own mind) that influences subsequent psychological development, not the objective status of the relationship. The external environment is hardly relevant compared to the child's fantasy world.

For Klein, the most important determinants of mental illness are pre-Oedipal events occurring in the very first year of life. As a result of this emphasis, her principal technical contribution to the psychoanalytic movement was child analysis. Even infants as young as two were considered appropriate for treatment. Of course, the very young cannot be restrained on the analyst's couch and requested to free-associate; however, they can be encouraged to participate in games, given toys with which to play, and asked to make up stories. What the child does and what the child says under these conditions can be interpreted in much the same way as the recollections of an adult.

As suggested earlier, Klein appears to be closer to the spirit of Freud than many other post-Freudians. Her willingness to continue his exploration of the destructive instinct, which others simply dismissed, is clear evidence of her loyalty. Moreover, Freud had always expressed an interest in the very earliest experiences and their effect on development. It should not be forgotten that he described birth as the first great anxiety state. He toyed with the idea that early separation experiences were traumatic and often wrote that fear of separation was a key feature of neurotic illness. Clearly, Klein's work represents a continuation of these themes.

Freud and Klein shared a deep conviction that a strong bond between mother and child was essential for healthy development and that the threat of loss or separation was likely to have negative consequences; however, in the writings of both of them, these ideas remain nothing more than speculative. They were never tested or proven. It was a British psychiatrist who was to continue exploring the links between the quality of early relationships and subsequent vulnerability to mental illness, and while doing so, make psychoanalytic ideas more respectable to the scientific establishment by collecting supportive evidence.

John Bowlby was born in 1907, the scion of a well-heeled British family. He was, therefore, somewhat removed from the internecine wars of the psychoanalytic movement. In the 1920s and early 1930s, when Anna Freud and Melanie Klein were locked in opposition, Bowlby was still a student; however, after studying and qualifying in medicine he chose to train as a psychoanalyst. Although he was never destined to enter the fray in quite the same way as his predecessors, he would be directly responsible for establishing a framework for future controversy and debate.

Bowlby agreed with Klein (who was at one time his supervisor) that links existed between psychiatric problems and the quality of early relationships; however, he was particularly interested in the effect of separation experiences, during which mother and child are forced to spend time apart. Unlike Klein, Bowlby was less concerned with the emotional consequences of childhood fantasies about separation. He was more interested in the emotional consequences of *actual* separation. His early work involved gathering information on the psychological well-being of children raised in institutions. Many of these unfortunate children not only experienced emotional difficulties, but also failed to thrive physically and do well at school. In 1952, Bowlby stated that 'maternal care in infancy and early childhood is essential for mental health'. This idea may now seem transparently obvious; however, in the 1950s Bowlby's work was considered highly original.

Bowlby's findings were summarized in a report for the World Health Organization; however, the contents of this report were presented in a book accessible to the interested layperson entitled *Child Care and the Growth of Love*. It is perhaps through this more popular vehicle that Bowlby's work came to be generally recognized and understood. Although subsequent research has led to frequent reassessment of Bowlby's work, and the detail is still subject to debate, there is widespread agreement with respect to his general conclusions.

For both the layperson and the professional, the name of John Bowlby has become connected with one term more than any other: *maternal deprivation*. He demonstrated that the absence of a loving relationship between mother and child, particularly in the first seven years of life, leaves the infant vulnerable with respect to the development of psychological problems such as anxiety and depression, as well as more complex social difficulties (for example, impaired ability to receive and give affection). The key difference between Freud and Bowlby is that whereas for the former the important instincts underlying psychological problems were sexual and aggressive, for the latter there is only one important issue: the need for *security*.

Subsequent to his work for the World Health Organization, Bowlby began to study the effects of maternal deprivation on young children more directly. This was usually achieved by the observation of children under conditions which required temporary separation from parents (for example, during a period of hospitalization). It is now well known that infants develop specific attachments in the second six months of the first year. If handed to a stranger, the young child will *protest*. It will cry and attempt to cling to its mother. Clearly, the child is anxious and unsettled by the unfamiliarity of the stranger. If the mother is removed altogether, then the protest phase will be followed by *despair*. The infant becomes miserable and wretched, behaving in much the same way as a depressed adult might. Should the period of separation from the mother be prolonged, despair is eventually replaced with *detachment*. It is as though the infant is unable to tolerate further distress and cuts off emotionally. This sequence of mental states – protest, despair and detachment – was proven to be a reliable phenomenon in small children separated from their mothers.

Bowlby's work on maternal deprivation, and later observations of children undergoing separation experiences, were eventually integrated within a general framework that has come to be known as *attachment theory*. It is within this general framework that the mechanisms linking early relationships and mental health can be properly understood. The psychiatrist and Bowlby biographer, Jeremy Holmes, suggests: 'Attachment theory is in essence a spatial theory: when I am close to my loved one I feel good, when I am far away I am anxious, sad or lonely.' In the child's world, 'mother' becomes what the psychologist Mary Ainsworth called a *secure base*. This sense of security gives the young child the confidence to act in ways consistent with its natural tendency to be curious. It is able to explore and acquire experience essential for healthy development. If an unusual or frightening situation develops, it knows that the 'attachment figure', mother, will be there to provide comfort and pro-tection. When the danger passes, exploration can continue.

Having observed the effects of maternal deprivation on

children, Bowlby began to consider the nature of mental processes that might link early separation experiences and problems in later life. He asked the simple question: 'What is happening in the child's mind?' Bowlby speculated that as a child develops, it constructs mental representations of itself and others. He described these representations as *internal working models*. Such models are based on repeated patterns of social experience. A securely attached child will store an internal working model of a responsive, loving and reliable caregiver. Moreover, a securely attached child will store a working model of itself that is worthy of love and attention. This latter working model might be described in everyday language as a 'good self-image'. Positive internal representations have a profound effect on the beliefs a child forms about relationships. Thus, the nature of the internal working model will influence the beliefs and expectations that the child brings to all other relationships, even those developed in adulthood.

An insecurely attached child is likely to construct internal working models very different to those of the securely attached child. He or she will view the world as a dangerous place in which people are to be treated with great caution. Moreover, he or she is likely to develop a 'poor self-image', of someone who is ineffective and unworthy of love. This insecurity may promote the use of defensive strategies which will only serve to compound the problem, much the same as defence mechanisms function in traditional Freudian psychology.

It is perhaps because Bowlby was somewhat removed from the battleground of the early psychoanalytic movement that he refrained from developing his own school of psychotherapy. He did not need to make a bold declaration of independence, at least not in the same way as predecessors like Adler, Jung and Klein. When Bowlby was writing up his first major study, Freud had been dead for over a decade; battles had begun to turn into skirmishes, and arguments into discussions. The climate was changing. Moreover, Bowlby was temperamentally ill-suited to head a 'Bowlbyan' school of psychotherapy. Biographers have remarked on his typically English temperament. He was a cool, sometimes remote, somewhat modest man; rallying the troops would have been an anathema to him. Yet Bowlby's failure to establish his own school has, ironically, proved his greatest asset. It is far easier to accept a man's ideas than the man himself. Subsequently, Bowlby's ideas have gained greater currency over the years than any of those promulgated by the early schismatics. Bowlby never demanded fealty, merely a hearing. And not surprisingly, given the humility of his request, he got it.

Bowlby's influence has extended well beyond the psychoanalytic movement. With respect to the practice of psychotherapy, Bowlby's contribution is twofold. Firstly, few contemporary therapists would argue with the idea that a secure attachment in early childhood helps to promote good mental health. Secondly, Bowlby's ideas suggest a common mechanism explaining the efficacy of all therapies, insofar as the therapeutic relationship provides the patient with experience of a secure base. The therapist, in effect, re-parents the patient, providing ideal conditions for the creation of good internal working models. Ideally, the patient leaves therapy having had experience of a reliable attachment figure, which in itself will increase self-esteem and self-worth. Inevitably, these psychological changes will reduce vulnerability to anxiety and depression. Although there is no such thing as a 'Bowlbyan therapist', almost all therapists are inadvertently 'Bowlbyans'.

In addition to influencing our understanding of how psychotherapy works, Bowlby has more or less single-handedly altered the course of child psychiatry. Even today, a large body of research, inspired by Bowlby, continues to develop and grow. Moreover, much of this research has had a direct influence on social policy and the decision-making processes that determine how child welfare issues are resolved. However, Bowlby's academic reputation rests on his novel insistence that psychoanalytic ideas should be examined with the detached eye of a scientist. Although Freud claimed to be scientist, he failed to undertake any large-scale studies. For him, the only evidence worth looking at was clinical evidence. This was something of a tactical error, and traditional psychoanalysis has never been embraced by the scientific community for this reason. Bowlby was a pragmatist. He saw the weak link in the psychoanalytic method and set about repairing it. He drew numerous strands of evidence together, even relevant work conducted on animals. Subsequently, attachment theory is one of the most well-supported concepts in psychology.

Since Bowlby, there has only been one other individual in the psychoanalytic tradition to achieve widespread influence. He is a figure who can be sharply contrasted with Bowlby, insofar as he sought to establish (and subsequently did so very successfully) his own school of psychotherapy. Eric Berne was, in many respects, the modern representative of the schismatic line. However, his treatment procedure, *transactional analysis* (often simply abbreviated to TA), has proved remarkably popular.

Eric Berne was born in Montreal in 1910. He studied medicine and went on to train as an analyst in New York. In the late 1950s and early 1960s, Berne began to publish work on a new form of psychoanalysis. It was strongly influenced by Freud and in many respects can be viewed as a populist account of Freudian ideas. Although traditional analysts would argue, perhaps rightly, that TA is largely plagiarism and over-simplification, Berne's ideas have a strong intuitive appeal.

The central concept in Berne's framework for understanding minds is the *ego state*. An ego state is a consistent pattern of feelings and thoughts that will correspond with a particular repertoire of behaviours. The ego state is both, a knowledge base (biasing how people act in certain situations) and a way of relating to others, a set of instructions and a 'role'.

According to Berne, individuals exhibit three types of ego state. He termed these *parent, adult* and *child*. In any social exchange, one of these ego states will predominate. A rough correspondence exists between Berne's parent, adult, and child and Freud's superego, ego and id.

The parental ego state, like the superego, reflects the attitude of parental figures. It has two forms: the *controlling* or *prejudicial* parent and the *nurturing* parent. The adult ego state is like the Freudian ego. When it predominates, the individual is able to appraise situations in an objective and accurate way and make appropriate judgements. The child ego state reflects feelings that are the relics of an individual's childhood. Like the parent ego state the child ego state has two forms: the *natural* or *healthy* child and the *adapted* child. The latter is a less healthy manifestation; it is characterized by feelings and behaviour which reflect a negative response to parental control, for example, sulking or being over-compliant.

Berne described the basic unit of social intercourse as a *transaction.* He suggested that transactions could be of three types: *complementary, converse* and *ulterior.* A complementary transaction occurs when the response to an initial statement or gesture is appropriate and expected. The transaction follows in a natural way. For example, two adults behaving foolishly and having fun together are enjoying a complementary transaction. They each understand why the other is choosing to behave immaturely. It could be said to be a child–child transaction; however, complementary transactions are not confined to social commerce between identical ego states. An individual might behave foolishly with the intention of eliciting a parental response from another adult. For example, a man behaving like a little boy might be seeking a maternal response from his wife. This appeal to his wife's maternal instinct may be satisfactory from her point of view. Their exchanges will run smoothly. This ease and facility of social behaviour is the defining feature of complementary transactions.

A *converse transaction* occurs when a response is returned from an ego state different from the one addressed. Moreover, the response might be directed at an ego state different to the one that initiated the transaction. The result of a converse transaction is that communication will be broken off. Berne gives the following example. A man's 'adult' signal to his 'adult' wife takes the form of a question: 'Do you know where my cuff links are?' The adult response might be: 'On the desk.' However, the wife might interpret the question as a criticism and reply: 'You always blame me for everything.' Such a response is a child–parent transaction. Berne suggests that transacting must realign before social exchanges can proceed without misunderstanding and tension.

Ulterior transactions are transactions with subtexts. They occur when, under the guise of an acceptable communication, an individual engages in a covert or socially risky communication.

Thus, an ulterior transaction has a hidden psychological agenda. It is, as it were, a wolf in sheep's clothing. The world of ulterior transaction was popularized by Berne in his book, *Games People Play*. Berne defined a 'game' as 'an ongoing series of complementary ulterior transactions progressing to a well defined, predictable outcome.' This predictable outcome usually takes the form of some kind of pay-off.

Berne detailed the manoeuvres and counter-manoeuvres of numerous games; however, 'The stocking game' will serve as a typical example. A woman, adept at playing this game, might enter a social situation and remark: 'Oh my, I have a run in my stockings.' This seemingly innocuous remark may draw attention to her legs. It is calculated to arouse the men who are present and make the women in the room angry. The aim of the game is to demonstrate that other people have lascivious minds; however, it might also provide the basic elements for an argument between married couples at a later stage in the evening.

The transactions that Berne describes in *Games People Play* are really an exhaustive account of varieties of transference. In the same way that a patient might come to view the analyst as a father figure in traditional psychoanalysis, so, Berne suggested, might similar distortions occur in everyday social situations. Thus, patterns of relating established in early life might be repeated in adulthood. The individual becomes locked into a way of dealing with people such that transactions tend to follow particular routines. An abused daughter may very easily become an abused wife. The stage props may change, but the submissive role remains the same.

The goals of TA are similar to the goals of traditional psychoanalysis. Freud's procedure was designed to reclaim portions of the id for the ego. In TA, the adult ego state must decide when to transact as parent or child. Moreover, it must be capable of resuming the adult ego state when necessary. If an individual does not have control of his or her ego states in social situations, others can consciously – or even unconsciously – activate his or her parent or child. This inevitably places the individual at a great disadvantage. Like traditional psychoanalysis, TA attempts to liberate the individual from the tyranny of past influences; however, unlike traditional psychoanalysis TA focuses almost exclusively on the social domain. Needless to say, the ideas of Alfred Adler almost certainly have shaped Berne's conception of human nature. TA is as much about striving for power as Adler's *individual psychology*, although this may be implicit rather than explicit in Berne's writings.

An important part of the technique of TA is the use of diagrams to help patients understand their ego states. They can be used to show how particular social situations can be analysed in terms of crossed and ulterior transactions. This use of diagrams has become a feature of many therapeutic approaches, even those that have developed outside the analytic tradition. It is as innovative, in its own way, as Jung's employment of art in the consulting room.

In the fifty or so years that span Adler's secession to the publication of *Games People Play*, psychoanalytic theory and practice had undergone considerable revision. Adler, Jung, Klein, Bowlby and Berne are arguably the most significant figures to have challenged or modified Freud's framework for understanding minds. There were, of course, many other figures who contributed to the development of psychoanalysis; however, their influence has not been substantial. Moreover, the peripheral schools have exhibited a clear tendency to drift towards either eccentric modes of practice or the endorsement of questionable therapeutic goals. For example, the European Existential school can be traced from the writings of Jean-Paul Sartre, through the clinical work of psychiatrists such as Ludwig Binswanger, to more contemporary figures such as R. D. Laing. An extreme, though revealing example of the clinical absurdities endorsed by this school can be drawn from Binswanger's casebook. He claimed that one of his patients, the now infamous Ellen West, was helped 'existentially' even though the existential choice that she made was to commit suicide! For most clinicians, Binswanger's definition of 'helping' seems so broad as to render the term meaningless. Similarly, the tenets of the Bioenergetic school, founded by Wilhelm Reich, would test the tolerance of even the most progressive thinker. This approach began as a form of psychoanalysis in which biological factors were given particular emphasis; however, Reich's final work is so florid as to make the worse excesses of Jungian mysticism seem pedestrian by comparison. He inferred the existence of a universal biological energy which he called the *orgone* and argued that the key to mental health was the orgasm. He made use of physical manipulation to release 'blocked energy'; however, probing the bodies of naked patients was also considered legitimate. He invented a machine called the orgone accumulator and claimed that it could treat any symptom or disease. In 1954, the American authorities ordered that all his books and writings should be burned; he was arrested, sentenced and shortly after died ignominiously in jail.

Others, such as Eric Fromm, made modest contributions to psychoanalysis, but his work is not associated with any major theoretical revision or modification of clinical technique. On the other hand, the writings of the French philosopher and psychiatrist, Jacques Lacan, are revolutionary; however, his works are so inaccessible as to beggar belief. In recent years, Lacan has attracted a devoted following among the intelligentsia (particularly so since better translations of his works are becoming available). Nevertheless, it is likely that he will eventually take his place in the pantheon of great thinkers, rather than achieve recognition as an influential therapist. Although Lacan's first major work was completed by 1932, there are still very few Lacanian analysts practising outside his native France.

Excluding the works of more peripheral schools and figures, the early schismatics and their more significant successors influenced psychoanalysis in the following key ways. Firstly, all mainstream psychoanalytic theorists since Freud have placed a weaker emphasis on the importance of the sex drive in understanding human motivation and the origins of mental illness. Secondly, many post-Freudians have underscored the importance of forming satisfactory relationships in early childhood. This shift might be considered as part of a greater awareness of the role of social factors in healthy emotional development. Thirdly, with the exception of Klein, most post-Freudians have afforded the conscious mind greater influence with respect to the development of psychological problems. Indeed, many of the post-Freudians described themselves as *ego analysts*. For them, the most important features of the mind were above the surface, not below. Finally, by the 1960s the practice of psychoanalysis had become somewhat different. Therapists had become less remote, assuming in sessions the 'character' of an interested friend or parent, rather than that of Freud's 'surgeon of the mind'. Attempts were also made to complete psychoanalysis in fewer sessions than the Olympian numbers advocated by Freud.

In spite of these trends and changes, it is difficult to understand why the psychoanalytic movement has, in overall terms, suffered from so many rifts and fractures. Even if factors such as personal animosity are excluded, most of those who broke with Freudian orthodoxy were not as radically opposed to Freud's ideas as they would have the world believe. Indeed, most of the 'revolutionary' ideas espoused by the post-Freudians, are, on closer examination, ideas that Freud himself had originally conceived, then discarded or neglected. In view of this, the fragmentation of the Freudian empire is even more mystifying than at first sight. Jung's collective unconscious is not too dissimilar to Freud's idea of an inherited 'archaic heritage'. Klein's work on *aggression* was almost certainly influenced by Freud's notion of the death instinct – Thanatos – which was introduced to explain destructive impulses. The seeds of Bowlby's work on the effects of separation experiences are to be found in Freud's description of birth trauma, and Berne's ego states are clearly a more accessible representation of Freud's trio of agencies that constitute the mind. It is perhaps only Alfred Adler, among the serried ranks of post-Freudians, whose precocious consideration of social factors in the origins of neurotic illness places him outside the Freudian orbit. The differences that fuelled years of internecine struggle in the psychoanalytic movement are diminished with hindsight. It is possible that this diminution of differences goes some way towards explaining why, by the 1960s, Freud's name was still synonymous with psychology and psychotherapy. A half century of betrayals, revisionists, *ad hominem* criticism – and not least of all his own death – had failed to topple the embattled founder from his pedestal.

It is often suggested that more words have been written about Sigmund Freud than any other human being, with the exception of Jesus Christ. This contention, if not entirely accurate, certainly conveys something of the extent to which Freud has become a cultural icon. Stefan Zweig's flattering affirmation that his friend's influence extended well beyond the development of a method for healing minds proved to be even more prophetic after Freud's death.

In the 1940s and 1950s, playwrights such as Eugene O'Neill and Tennessee Williams devised characters who were vehicles for the exploration of psychoanalytic ideas. Indeed, for a time, Broadway hosted numerous productions that drew their inspiration from psychoanalysis. Remarkably, the influence of Freud's thinking was not limited to serious drama. Popular shows such as *The Seven Year Itch* and *Lady in the Dark* also owed a debt to psychoanalytic ideas. Even cinema, that most popular of art forms, was forced to concede. Alfred Hitchcock's *Spellbound* married the seemingly incompatible genres of the medical case history and the murder mystery to produce the world's first psychoanalytic thriller. In this film, the main protagonists consult a sage analyst, who, in all but name, is Sigmund Freud. The most remarkable tribute to Freud to hail from Hollywood, however, is John Huston's 1962 film, *Freud, the Secret Passion*. It is a piece of shameless hagiography, portraying Freud as a fearless prophet, descending into the underworld and returning to liberate mankind from ignorance. Had he lived to see it, Carl Gustav Jung would have almost certainly recognized the unmistakable leitmotif of the sun-hero myth. Even Freud, who was prone to self-aggrandizement, would never have expected such extravagant praise. Although in life Freud was never to achieve his childhood dream of becoming a new Hannibal, in death he became just such a hero on the big screen.

By the 1960s, Freud's position as the founder of a new branch of clinical practice and a cultural figure seemed unassailable. He had seen off virtually all of the home-grown competition. Moreover, his extraordinary, sometimes implausible ideas about the origins of mental illness and the workings of the mind had somehow become settled in the popular imagination. Yet, while the early analysts had been debating the primacy of sexual over aggressive instincts, conscious over unconscious processes and Oedipal over pre-Oedipal complexes, a threat to the entire psychoanalytic edifice had been slowly fermenting. While psychoanalysts had been viewing each other with suspicion, the real enemy had already begun a painfully slow advance. In fact, even while Freud and his young colleagues sat in the cigar smoke-filled salon of Bergasse 19, forging the metal of their new 'science', an entirely different approach to understanding the mind was beginning to develop in Russia. A book by a physiologist, with the inauspicious title of *The Work of the Digestive Glands*, was published the same year that Freud presided over the first meeting of the Wednesday-night club. Little did its author realize, that this volume would lead to a programme of truly revolutionary research, the results of which would change the face of psychotherapy. However, such changes would not occur for nearly sixty years. Freud and his colleagues could afford to squabble and fight.

CHAPTER 4

The Exiled Mind

'Am I just to be like a clockwork orange?'
Anthony Burgess, *A Clockwork Orange*

In 1822, a young French-Canadian trapper called Alexis St
Martin was accidentally shot. A US army surgeon, William
Beaumont, arrived to examine his ailing patient and found that
the 'duck shot' had 'entered posteriorly', damaging muscles,
ribs and lungs, before 'perforating the stomach'. Not
surprisingly, Beaumont thought that St Martin would die. Yet,
after two years of nursing, the young man made a full recovery.
A full recovery, that is, with the exception of one detail. St
Martin's perforated stomach never fully healed. A fleshy 'lid'
had formed over the wound, which could be lifted so as to allow
direct observation of the process of digestion. Beaumont
undertook a series of extraordinary experiments in which
pieces of food, attached to a string, were repeatedly introduced
into, and removed from, St Martin's stomach. The hitherto
secret processes that governed digestion were, for the first
time, revealed. When St Martin's career as a human laboratory
ended, he married, fathered four children and became a
sergeant in the US army. William Beaumont, on the other
hand, swiftly achieved eminence as a scientist of considerable
importance. His opus on digestion established a benchmark
for work in this field, most notably for Ivan Petrovich Pavlov,
professor of physiology at St Petersburg's Military Medical
Academy.

Pavlov had recognized that, although Beaumont's
experiments were ingenious and revolutionary, contemporary

science required a more systematic examination of digestive processes. Such detailed study could only be undertaken using animals as experimental subjects. In Pavlov's laboratory, fistulas or 'openings' were surgically created along the digestive tract of dogs, so that chemical reactions could be observed directly after feeding – in much the same way as Beaumont was able to do with St Martin, although without the limitation of a single aperture. This kind of work had been attempted many times before without success. Usually the experimental animals died. This did not happen in Pavlov's laboratory as he is reputed to have employed a surgeon who found the sight of blood intolerable. A consequence of this possibly unique attribute among surgeons was that tissue damage during operations was reduced to an absolute minimum. Pavlov's findings were summarized in his book, *The Work of the Digestive Glands*. It was published in 1904, the same year in which he was awarded the Nobel Prize for physiology.

While undertaking this distinguished programme of research, Pavlov had noticed something rather odd about his dogs. Something that might have easily been overlooked. He had been conducting a series of experiments on the *salivary reflex*. In Pavlov's time, a reflex was thought to be an innate, automatic response to a given stimulus. The experimental procedure had involved placing a dog in harness and inducing salivation by squirting a mild acid solution into the dog's mouth. This procedure was repeated on several occasions. Pavlov's perplexing observation was that once dogs had become accustomed to the experimental procedure, simply producing the apparatus triggered salivation. It appeared to Pavlov that their mouths were 'watering' in anticipation. This observation was perplexing, because the salivatory reflex, a supposedly innate and automatic response, was being produced as a result of prior experience or learning. Pavlov described the salivation that resulted from prior experience as *psychic secretion*.

Pavlov believed that the study of psychic secretions might prove to be an interesting new line of research; however, he was reluctant to investigate the phenomenon any further because it appeared to be very psychological in nature. Dogs seemed to be 'remembering' what had happened to them in the past and also seemed to be able to use this knowledge to predict the administration of the acid solution. The idea of conducting a programme of psychological research made Pavlov very uneasy. This was not because, as a physiologist, he felt unqualified or at a disadvantage. The laboratory methods he had developed while studying digestion would be ideal for studying *learned reflexes*. He simply thought that psychology wasn't much of a discipline. Indeed, he once wrote that it is 'open to question whether psychology is a natural science, or whether it can be regarded as a science at all'.

When after some deliberation, Pavlov finally turned his attention to the systematic study of psychic secretions, he developed a simple experimental procedure that demonstrated a reflex could be 'taught'. A bell was rung just prior to dogs receiving food. This was repeated several times. After several repetitions, Pavlov discovered that his dogs would salivate as soon as the bell was rung. A neutral stimulus, that is a bell ring, had acquired a property formerly associated with food presentation. A reflex had been taught. The term used to describe this process was *conditioning*. It is now usually distinguished from other forms of conditioning by routine use of the prefix *classical*. Once an animal is conditioned, the conditioning will not last indefinitely. When pairings of bell and food are stopped, salivation in response to bell ringing will eventually diminish and finally cease altogether. When this occurs, the conditioned response is said to have become *extinguished*.

A quite complicated vocabulary has been developed to describe the elements of the classical conditioning procedure. Because food is able to trigger salivation before conditioning occurs, it is called the *unconditioned stimulus* (UCS). The salivation itself is described as the *unconditioned response* (UCR). After conditioning, the bell alone triggers salivation. The bell is thus called the *conditioned stimulus* (CS), while the salivation acquires a new name and is subsequently called the *conditioned response* (CR). Unfortunately, this sometimes confusing terminology has become the lingua franca of psychologists working in this area.

Although Pavlov is said to have been hopelessly sentimental

and even absent-minded outside work, his personality changed in the laboratory. He seemed to combine reptilian patience with machine-like intelligence, a union of attributes ideally suited to the demands of his work. He would systematically vary experimental stimuli, the number of UCS and CS pairings, and then closely observe the varying strengths of conditioned reflexes. Pavlov was so meticulous that he was soon able to formulate the fundamental laws that governed classical conditioning. He thus not only discovered the process, but also virtually exhausted its possibilities in the laboratory.

Pavlov discovered that conditioning was more successful when the interval between the bell ring (CS) and the food presentation (UCS) was short; however, if the food was presented before the bell ring, conditioning could not be achieved, no matter how brief the presentation interval. He discovered that the conditioned stimulus can share its 'power' to elicit a conditioned response if paired with another stimulus. For example, a bell ring would precede oral administration of a mild acid solution to produce salivation. The bell would then be paired with a light. After repeated pairings of bell and light, presentation of the light alone would cause the animal to salivate. This phenomenon Pavlov called *higher order conditioning*.

He discovered that conditioned reflexes could be elicited by similar, but not identical stimuli to the original conditioned stimulus. For example, if a dog were conditioned to salivate to a tone, slightly higher or lower pitches would also elicit salivation; however, the amount the dog would salivate was inversely related to the discrepancy between the pitch of the original and subsequent tones. This phenomenon of salivating to 'near relatives' of the original conditioned stimulus Pavlov called *generalization*.

With his characteristic attention to detail, Pavlov continued to explore the parameters of classical conditioning; however, some unexpected events in the laboratory started him wondering about the origins of mental illness. These unexpected events occurred in the context of two sets of experiments.

In the first set of experiments, a dog was conditioned to

salivate on presentation of a circle. This stimulus was then alternated with an ellipse of similar size. At first, the salivation response *generalized*. That is, the dog salivated in response to both figures; however, if each further presentation of the circle was associated with a splash of acid on the tongue (to encourage salivation), and each further presentation of the ellipse was not associated with a splash of acid, then salivation in response to the ellipse diminished and finally disappeared altogether. The dog had learned to *differentiate* between the circle and the ellipse.

The second set of experiments took this paradigm into new and exciting territory. Although these experiments took place in Pavlov's laboratory, they were originally reported by Shenger-Krestovnika in 1921. First, a dog was taught to differentiate a circle from a long elliptical figure in the usual way; however, when the dog stopped salivating in response to ellipse presentation, a slightly less oblong ellipse was presented instead. In other words, it was a more 'circular' ellipse, possessing just enough 'circularity' to trigger salivation. Again, the animal was taught to differentiate circle from ellipse, and when this was successfully achieved, an even more 'circular' ellipse was introduced into the procedure. This process would continue for some time; that is, until the ellipse figure became almost circular. Then something very odd happened. Normally placid dogs became extremely agitated. They howled, barked and struggled to be free of their restraining harnesses. When released from the apparatus, they were almost impossible to handle for hours after the experiment. If these traumatized dogs were brought back to be given easier discrimination tasks, they failed. It was as though they had become psychologically disturbed. Pavlov saw similarities between what had happened to these laboratory dogs and the behaviour of humans during a nervous breakdown. Subsequently, he described the distress caused by the differentiation task as an *experimental neurosis*.

Reflecting on the exact nature of the distress observed in these animals, Pavlov considered the key cause of an 'experimental neurosis' to be unavoidable conflict. The conflict generated in Shenger-Krestovnika's study involved two strong but incompatible conditioned responses: either to salivate, or to suppress salivation on presentation of an ambiguous ellipse. It is as though the animal experiences something very similar to what a human might experience if forced to struggle with an insoluble problem or dilemma to which there is no obvious answer. Freud, of course, placed conflict at the heart of the psychoanalytic account of neurotic illness, particularly the conflict between libidinal urges generated by the id and the moral prohibitions of the superego. It is interesting that the concept of conflict should find a central role in Pavlov's account of neurotic illness, even though his work was undertaken in a physiological laboratory, rather than bourgeois Vienna.

Although Pavlov speculated about the relationship between the behaviour of his laboratory animals and mental illness, it was not until 1929, at the age of 80, that he devoted his attention fully to the problem of human psychopathology; however, he made surprisingly little use of the concept of classical conditioning. Instead, he chose to explain mental illness in terms of biological factors such as the characteristics of the nervous system. Pavlov believed that people were born with different temperaments. Moreover, these temperaments were determined by the strength and weakness of nerve cells, particularly those that make up the outer layer (or cortex) of the brain. Individuals with certain brain types are therefore predisposed to develop specific types of mental illness in response to stress, particularly stress, involving conflict. Bearing in mind the emphasis Pavlov gave to biological factors, the treatments that he recommended were physical rather than psychological, for example, drugs such as bromide.

Pavlov died a national hero; it was a truly astonishing achievement for a man whose family had once eked out a peasant-style existence in a Russian farming village. Even a town was named after him. Moreover, his views on the biological nature of the mind and mental illness were championed by the Soviet political establishment. Pavlov's work suggested that man was little more than an organic machine. This was a view that was particularly attractive to those wishing to diminish the importance of individuality while extolling the virtues of the collective. He was hailed as the founder of a new Marxist psychology. The messy and decadent world of Freud's psychoanalysis was utterly rejected, to be replaced by a clear-minded, scientific understanding of human suffering, in which sadness and fear could be reduced to abnormal chemical activity on the surface of the brain – chemical activity that would one day be corrected with medication and other physical treatments.

Pavlov's work and ideas exercised a profound influence on the course of Soviet psychiatry, which subsequently always favoured a biological account of human suffering. It is very likely that Pavlov himself would have approved of this. After all, he had always rejected 'psychology'; however, he was destined to become the hapless victim of history. Ironically, Pavlov the physiologist and brain scientist would be remembered outside his own country, more than anything else, as Pavlov the psychologist. Moreover, he would, in time, become the patron saint of a movement in psychology whose membership would show little interest in the biological determinants of mental illness. And, as if this were not enough, the clinical significance of his work would not be recognized by psychiatrists and neurologists sharing his reductionist views, but rather, by 'psychotherapists'. It is inconceivable that, if they met, Fate and Pavlov could ever be on speaking terms.

The group who canonized Pavlov, and thus secured his place in the history books as a psychologist, were the *behaviourists*. The ideology of behaviourism, was baldly stated in an article published in 1913 by the movement's founding father, John Broadus Watson (then professor of psychology at Johns Hopkins University). It appeared in the academic journal *Psychological Review*, which Watson also edited. This article, entitled 'Psychology as the behaviourist views it', is nothing less than a manifesto. It contains two very revealing statements. Watson writes: 'Psychology as the behaviourist views it is a purely objective natural science'. Thus, he believed that speculating about internal mental events and their meaning was an entirely fruitless endeavour. Such mental events could not be observed, making them inaccessible and therefore unfit for scientific study. Only 'behaviour' could be observed. This represents perhaps the most extraordinary policy statement ever issued in the history of a scientific discipline. Watson had suggested that psychologists should stop studying the mind. In effect, psychology should exile its principal protagonist.

Watson's second telling statement on the nature of behaviourism was: 'Its theoretical goal is the prediction and control of behaviour.' Psychology, therefore, should be an applied science. Once the laws that governed behaviour were fully understood, then they would be put to use in schools, hospitals and the home. Behaviourism was not an ideology for the faint-hearted. Displaying what can only be described as frontier spirit, Watson openly declared his intention to change the world.

It wasn't until Watson had written his manifesto that he began to make use of Pavlovian ideas, particularly so with respect to understanding the origins of phobias, the irrational fears that feature so significantly in the psychoanalytic literature. Watson suggested that phobias might be the result of conditioning experiences. For example, fear might be the natural emotional response to being trapped. If an individual becomes frightened on account of being trapped in an elevator, then such an individual may develop a conditioned fear of lifts. In Pavlovian jargon it can be said that the UCR (fear), has been paired with a CS (the lift), which now has the power to elicit fear as a CR (that is, a conditioned response). Just seeing a lift will now activate the muscles and glands responsible for feelings of tension and anxiety. Once Watson had developed his Pavlovian account of phobias, he then set about demonstrating its validity.

In 1920, a paper entitled 'Conditioned emotional reactions' appeared in the *Journal of Experimental Psychology*. It was written by Watson and one of his students, Rosalie Rayner. Even today, it remains one of the most controversial publications in the history of psychology; however, it also marks a turning point, the juncture at which behaviourism rose to meet the challenge of its manifesto and began translating theory into practice.

The subject of Watson and Rayner's experiment was the 11-month-old son of a hospital worker, Albert B. He is now immortalized in textbooks on behaviourism as Little Albert and presented as something of a foil to a famous case of Freud's known as Little Hans. The latter was a five-year-old child whose phobia of horses was attributed to Oedipal conflicts. Watson and Rayner set out to show that such irrational fears were not the result of complex unconscious processes and the operation of defence mechanisms, but instead, straightforward classical conditioning.

Little Albert was first shown a white rat, to which he responded with some interest; however, whenever Albert reached out to touch the animal, a loud noise was produced by striking a steel bar with a hammer situated just behind his head. Understandably, this caused the infant considerable distress. After subsequent pairings of the rat and the loud noise, Albert showed symptoms of distress, even when the rat was produced without its cacophonous accompaniment. The rat had ceased to become an interesting creature and was now a CS capable of evoking anxiety. Albert's fear obeyed Pavlovian laws, and promptly 'generalized' to a range of 'furry' stimuli. He would whimper when confronted with a rabbit, a dog, cotton wool and even a Santa Claus mask. Watson and Rayner tested Little Albert a month after completing their conditioning procedure. They were delighted to find the infant's fears were unchanged. They never saw him again.

Watson and Rayner made absolutely no attempt to de-condition Little Albert. Yet, in their paper they had suggested a number of methods that might easily have achieved this end. For example, one method might have been by repeated pairing of the rat with a pleasant stimulus such as candy (a technique known as counter-conditioning and familiar to Pavlov's research team). Yet more perplexing is the way Watson and Rayner chose to end their article. They speculated how, perhaps, some twenty years after their study, Little Albert might enter psychoanalysis. His dreams would be analysed and it might be concluded that his phobia was caused by early experiences of being punished for attempting to touch his mother's genitals!

Although Watson and Rayner's study was, by today's standards, almost wholly inexcusable on ethical grounds, it had many implications for the better understanding and treatment of anxiety disorders. For the very first time, a phobia had been created in the laboratory. Little Albert's irrational fear owed nothing to repression, forbidden wishes or Oedipal conflicts. It was merely the result of classical conditioning. Therefore, what had been learned could be unlearned. Pavlov had never truly grasped the clinical applications of his own work. Watson had no such problem.

Perhaps it was because Watson was so confident that phobias could be cured by counter-conditioning that he felt no obligation to prove it. Thus, Little Albert was prematurely abandoned. Fortunately, another psychologist, Mary C. Jones, picked matters up where Watson left off. In 1924, she demonstrated that if a feared object is repeatedly paired with a pleasant experience such as eating, it will eventually lose its power to frighten a child. Phobias, the most common of all psychological problems, had been stripped of their mystery.

Watson had married into a prominent political family and Rayner's parents were also public figures. When Watson's wife discovered that her husband was having an affair with his young student, a scandal was inevitable. Watson was forced to resign his chair at Johns Hopkins and the author of the behaviourist manifesto was, quite suddenly, jobless. Whereas others might have accepted defeat at this point, adverse circumstances hardly broke Watson's stride. He married Rayner and then joined the J. Walter Thompson Advertising Agency. He quadrupled his professor's salary and in four years was appointed vice-president. In his spare time he wrote popular magazine articles on psychology.

In 1928, only four years after the birth of his second son, Watson published a book entitled *Psychological Care of Infant and Child*, a manual for parents that sold extremely well. He explained how raising children could be successfully accomplished according to behavioural principles. These were principles that he had also employed raising his own two sons. Watson suggested that children should always be treated like adults. He wrote: 'Never hug and kiss them, never let them sit on your lap.' He recommended that every effort should be made to raise children as autonomous, self-reliant individuals. Coddling of any kind was considered unforgivable. One of Watson's sons became a psychologist, the other a psychiatrist.

The psychologist suffered from depression and was helped by a psychoanalyst. The psychiatrist also suffered from depression; however, he sadly committed suicide in 1963.

Although Watson had proved time and time again that he was in possession of a first-rate intellect, his ideas on child rearing were profoundly ill-conceived. Behavioural principles, applied indiscriminately, could easily arouse public disapproval. It was a salutary lesson that Watson's successors would ignore at their peril.

In spite of the Little Albert experiment, and the subsequent therapeutic work of Mary C. Jones, clinical practice remained remarkably unchanged. The revolutionary account of phobias that Watson had promoted was acknowledged, ignored, then largely forgotten. The average phobic patient in the 1920s and 1930s was just as likely to find him- or herself reclining on a psychoanalyst's couch, recalling dreams. Regardless of Watson's rhetoric, the Freudian empire held fast. There was, however, the exception of one outpost: enuresis.

The term enuresis is used to describe persistent childhood bed-wetting. Usually, no physical cause is detectable, and for an unlucky few, bed-wetting may continue into adolescence and adulthood. Needless to say, those afflicted suffer almost intolerable levels of shame and embarrassment. Although enuresis was considered a psychological problem, psychoanalysis was, on the whole, ineffective. Indeed, it fared little better than misplaced medical procedures, the worst example of which was bladder surgery. The behavioural solution to enuresis was remarkably simple. It is routinely described as the *standard conditioning method* and was introduced by a husband-and-wife team of psychologists, O. H. and W. M. Mowrer, in 1938. It was the first behavioural treatment to become generally accepted.

The Mowrers suggested that enuresis was not caused by a physical problem or repressed sexual drive, but by a straightforward failure to learn an appropriate response. The enuretic child must learn to control the voiding reflex when the bladder is full and wake up so that the bladder can be emptied. To this end, a device called the *bed-pad and alarm* was employed. A moisture sensitive pad is placed under the bed sheet (or in the child's pyjamas). This is connected to a battery-operated alarm such as a bell or buzzer. When the child urinates, the alarm sounds. Usually, the child wakes and stops urinating automatically. With repeated practice, the child is conditioned to respond to a full bladder by inhibiting urination and waking up. These two responses represent Pavlovian-learned reflexes. Once these reflexes have been thoroughly conditioned, the alarm system is no longer required and the child is able to enjoy complete continence throughout the night.

The therapeutic potential of nocturnal alarm systems had, in fact, been recognized since the turn of the twentieth century, most notably by a now largely forgotten German physician named Pfaundler. There are, perhaps, two reasons why the Mowrers' 1938 article proved influential. Firstly, the bell-pad and alarm was, and still is, a very convenient piece of technical apparatus. Secondly, the Mowrers' explanation of how the bell-pad and alarm works was wholly convincing. The combination of a user-friendly technology and a credible, scientific rationale was a winning one. It appealed to clinicians in a way that Watson's rather messy counter-conditioning procedure (employing food or candy) did not. Thus, the bell-pad and alarm became established as the first widely utilized behavioural therapy. As a result of the Mowrers' simple treatment, generations of schoolchildren were spared not only the misery of enuresis, but also profitless hours in the company of a psychoanalyst.

Remarkably, there were no further advances in clinical practice for many years. Behaviourism, irrespective of Watson's pragmatic manifesto, simply returned to the laboratory. The next major development was, therefore, as seemingly irrelevant to clinical practice as Pavlov's salivating dogs. Nevertheless, it was in fact of equal significance: the discovery and investigation of a second method of conditioning.

Most of the seminal research concerning what came to be known as *operant* or *instrumental conditioning* took place in the 1930s and 1940s; however, operant-conditioning phenomena had been observed before the turn of the century. Indeed, it is only because of delayed interest in operant conditioning that classical conditioning has acquired a prefix suggesting seniority. In the late 1890s, Edward Thorndike, then a graduate student at Columbia University, was studying *animal intelligence*. He found that when alley cats were confined in a cage, they would make frequent efforts to escape. Many of these attempts were futile; however, eventually, and purely by accident, a latch would be knocked and the cage door would open. If these feline Houndinis were returned to captivity, they would swiftly repeat their successful method of escape. As a result of these and subsequent observations, Thorndike formulated a simple principle of behaviour that he called the Law of Effect. Any behaviour that is followed by a rewarding consequence is likely to be repeated. The opposite is also true, insofar as behaviour followed by unpleasant consequences is more likely to diminish.

The idea that behaviour could be modified according to environmental *contingencies* was not really given further consideration until the late 1920s; however, in the laboratory of Burrhus Frederic Skinner, Thorndike's observations would be refined and developed, the outcome of which would be a comprehensive description of the principles governing operant conditioning. The term operant was used, because unlike classical conditioning, which is a largely passive process, operant conditioning requires the subject to operate some feature of the environment. Skinner's work gained momentum over subsequent decades, and by the 1950s he had established a body of work that had been collected with such scrupulous attention to detail that a comparison with Pavlov was inevitable.

Like Pavlov, Skinner's experimental subjects were animals, mostly pigeons and rats. In order to study their behaviour closely, Skinner invented a special piece of apparatus that is now known as the *Skinner box*. Essentially, this is a small cage in which an animal's behaviour can be rewarded or punished while a continuous record of events is kept on a moving roll of paper. This continuous record allowed Skinner to analyse animal behaviour with such precision that he was subsequently able to generate 'laws' of behaviour that could be expressed in mathematical formulae. Under Skinner's stewardship, psychology was becoming an altogether more respectable science.

In the same way that a new technical vocabulary became necessary to describe the elements of classical conditioning, so it was that operant conditioning also acquired its own unique lexicon. Thorndike had already established that pleasant or unpleasant consequences would increase or decrease the occurrence of prior behaviour in animals. In Skinner's vocabulary, pleasant and unpleasant consequences were respectively described as *positive reinforcement* and *punishment*; however, Skinner also discovered that behaviour could be influenced when expected consequences, both negative and positive, fail to happen. For example, a particular behaviour will increase in frequency if it becomes associated with the termination of an ongoing unpleasant stimulus (for example, switching off a previously continuous weak electric current). Skinner described this as *negative reinforcement*. Finally, he found that behaviour will decrease if an expected reward is withdrawn. He described this as *frustrative non-reward*.

Using these basic elements, Skinner was able to modify and shape the behaviour of his laboratory animals to an extraordinary degree. For example, Pigeons were taught to play ping-pong. It seemed that much of animal behaviour, and by inference much of human behaviour too, might be little more than a set of learned *habits*, entirely dependent on environmental contingencies; and surely, if a pigeon could be taught to play ping-pong, a disturbed psychiatric patient might also be taught to behave in a more socially acceptable manner. Theoretically, all that one had to do was make sure that desirable behaviours were rewarded, while undesirable behaviours were ignored. Yet, once again, behaviourism failed to do justice to Watson's manifesto. Although it was readily apparent that Skinner's method of modifying animal behaviour might also be used to modify the behaviour of psychiatric patients, nothing of the sort happened.

Given the halting, faltering, almost inconsequential progress of behaviourism in the clinic, it can only be assumed that the climate of ideas had, as yet, been unfavourable for the widespread acceptance of *behaviour therapy*. It has already been suggested that throughout the nineteenth century, philosophers and writers had been exploring concepts that would one day be united under the banner of psychoanalysis. Freud's timing could not have been better. Until the 1950s, the prevailing view of the mind and how it works was still essentially nineteenth century in nature. In hospitals and clinics, practitioners were unwilling to relinquish their received orthodoxy. Moreover, between 1900 and 1950, the psycho-analytic movement had expanded with such speed and ferocity that alternative methods of treatment were destined to be lost in the groundswell. Little Albert and his contemporaries were simply trampled under foot as Freud's troops made their noisy advance on the intellectual capitals of the twentieth century; however, by the 1950s, the initial momentum of psychoanalysis was beginning to flag. And, more importantly, in an atmosphere of post-war optimism, the world was becoming more receptive to new ideas.

American television commercials of the 1950s show science invading the home: a world of vacuum cleaners, refrigerators and labour-saving devices. Outside the home, the family car celebrated engineering with polished chrome and leather. Modern architecture was dispensing with unnecessary decoration. Science fiction had entered a golden age, predicting the imminent arrival of a cleaner world: a world of robots and computers, white towers and monorails; a world in which lives would run smoothly. After the chaos of the Second World War, a well-ordered society seemed no bad thing. Words such as clockwork and mechanistic began to sound reassuring, rather than soulless. If, as the behaviourists had been suggesting, man is nothing more than a type of machine, then this too might not be so bad. The intellectual climate of the world had changed, and psychology, as *behavioural science*, was looking like an attractive and more rational alternative to the restless passions that boiled in the Freudian id.

The 1950s were also a time in which psychoanalysis received its first major blow from an outside agency. The British psychologist Hans Eysenck published a highly influential paper in 1952, showing that being in psychoanalysis was no more beneficial than being on a waiting list for treatment. Subsequently, Eysenck claimed that roughly two-thirds of 'neurotic' patients recovered or improved to a marked extent within two years of the first episode of anxiety or depression. Therefore, those who entered lengthy Freudian psychoanalysis might appear to be benefiting from the treatment, when in fact they would have improved anyway. Eysenck's paper was followed by a series of articles that cast considerable doubt over the effectiveness of psychoanalysis. Although his conclusions were the subject of much heated debate – a debate which still rages in some circles – psychoanalysis had been dealt a powerful blow. The times then were propitious for change.

Joseph Wolpe, a psychiatrist living and working in South Africa, had become interested in conditioned fear. He had undertaken a series of experiments using cats as subjects. These were based on the counter-conditioning paradigm, and were part of a now established tradition extending back to Pavlov's laboratory, via Watson, Rayner and Mary C. Jones. Wolpe confirmed previous findings. Animals were conditioned to become fearful of certain stimuli; however, when these same stimuli were later paired with food, they soon ceased to evoke fear. Wolpe was very much interested in understanding why this phenomenon occurred and postulated that the act of eating actually *inhibited* the symptoms of fear. His next step was to consider how these laboratory findings might be used to treat anxiety problems in humans.

Although eating might well inhibit fear, Wolpe was not convinced that food could be readily incorporated into clinical practice. Psychotherapists had routinely made use of tasteful accessories such as the chaise longue or couch, usually placed in a book-lined study. Replacing these rather impressive props with a sandwich and chocolates seemed, no doubt, lacking in gravitas. Wolpe considered a wide range of potential alternatives to food as an inhibitory device; however, he finally selected an abbreviated version of *progressive muscular relaxation*. This procedure, originally developed by Edmund Jacobson in 1929, requires the patient to first tense, and then release, separate muscle groups. For example, the patient would clench the right hand tightly to produce a fist, then slowly release the grip. The procedure is undertaken in a systematic way so that all parts of the body are affected.

When given these instructions, patients are usually able to achieve a state of deep relaxation. With practice, this state can be deepened further. Once the skill of deep relaxation has been acquired, a patient might then be able to enter such a state with very little effort. Wolpe believed that relaxation training and eating both produced a similar effect on the nervous system; thus, relaxation could be used in place of food as a convenient method of inhibiting fear. Although this is not strictly true, relaxation became an important feature of Wolpe's new method for treating anxiety.

After Wolpe's patients had acquired relaxation skills, they were then asked to construct a list (or *hierarchy*) of situations, ordered in such a way as to reflect increasing levels of anxiety. Patients were then encouraged to enter the situation appearing lowest on their list, that is, the situation associated with the least discomfort. Such modest levels of anxiety could be 'inhibited' with relative ease through relaxation. Once anxiety associated with the first item had been successfully inhibited, the procedure was repeated with respect to the second item, and so on, until all situations on the list had been dealt with. Using these simple guidelines, an individual with an irrational fear of spiders might begin treatment by inhibiting anxiety in the presence of a tiny specimen contained in a jar, and over time, be able to accomplish the same feat with a much larger relative. Little by little, Wolpe's patients learned to crowd out fear.

This procedure was excellent for patients whose irrational fears concerned a particular object or thing. Tasks of increasing difficulty were easy to specify, for example, slowly approaching a captive animal or insect. There were, however, many patients who reported anxiety that could not be linked with a specific object, for example, fear of failure or of criticism. Although it might be possible to practise the graded inhibition exercises in the presence of a captive spider, this kind of practice was not possible when fears were of a more abstract nature. Wolpe's solution to this problem was very simple. He asked his patients to simply *imagine* such situations, instead of attempting to enter them in real life. All of the other features of the inhibition procedure remained unchanged. Graded confrontation of anxiety-provoking situations in imagination became known as *systematic desensitization.*

Wolpe's procedure was found to be a highly effective treatment for anxiety. Re-creating feared situations in the mind, and then relaxing, seemed to help patients deal with those same situations when they occurred again in reality. Moreover, Wolpe found that desensitization in imagination worked as well for patients with specific fears (such as spiders) as it did for those with more abstract fears (such as failure). Wolpe's final version of his treatment involved a combination of *imaginal* and *in vivo* desensitization exercises. The former were undertaken in sessions with a therapist, while the latter were undertaken in real life by the patient alone, in the form of homework assignments. In 1958, Wolpe published his findings in a book entitled *Psychotherapy by Reciprocal Inhibition*. A therapy based on behavioural principles had again been presented to the world; however, this time, it was far from ignored.

Although Wolpe's systematic desensitization was welcomed as a swift and eminently practical approach to the treatment of anxiety problems, his book was viewed as pure heresy in some quarters. The squabbling psychoanalytic movement, united this time by the appearance of a serious common enemy, turned on Wolpe instantly. The criticism he received was harsh, personal and abusive. Hans Eysenck, reflecting on the behaviour of Wolpe's psychoanalytic colleagues, wrote: 'Their income, their status, their very *raison d'être* was at stake, so naturally they fought like hell . . .' However, the strength of their feeling is perhaps better understood as a protest in response to trespass. Wolpe's technique of systematic desensitization was devised to treat anxiety problems – the very problems that Freud had rescued from obscurity and given a central position in contemporary psychiatry. Wolpe was not only promoting a new approach to treatment, he was also doing so on Freud's holy ground.

The fact that behaviour therapy developed within a strong scientific tradition goes some way towards explaining why its practitioners were unable to accept that systematic desensitization worked, without asking further questions. Did people really get better because of counter-conditioning, or could the effectiveness of this technique be explained in other ways? After numerous investigations it was established that the critical feature of systematic desensitization was *exposure*, be that in imagination or reality, to the feared object or situation. The graded hierarchy could make the process of confronting fear less traumatic; however, even when phobic individuals were forced to face the top-most items on their hierarchies, anxiety would typically diminish within a single therapy session. This rather pitiless strategy is sometimes referred to as *flooding*. Although the time taken for anxiety to subside varied from individual to individual, most would report a steady decrease in fearfulness over a period of approximately 30 minutes to an hour. Further, the more time that patients spent confronting their anxiety, the more swiftly their phobias disappeared. Relaxation appeared to have no real function during systematic desensitization. Anxiety would diminish anyway, irrespective of whether an individual relaxed or not. The key element then was exposure.

This new insight required a new explanation. Wolpe had assumed that anxiety diminished because of the inhibitory effects of relaxation; however, this was now known to be wrong. Inhibition was thus abandoned, to be replaced by the concept of *habituation*. Essentially, habituation occurs when the nervous system becomes accustomed to a repeated stimulus and stops responding. In the 1960s and 1970s, habituation was a well-recognised phenomenon that had been languishing in textbooks, mostly on the nervous systems of invertebrates and other living systems; however, humans are experiencing habituation to a greater or lesser extent all of the time. When an individual walks into a room containing a loud clock, he or she might notice the ticking sound. If he or she remains in this room, the ticking sound will gradually fade from awareness (unless attention is drawn to it again). The nervous system has simply become used to the sound, and those parts responsible for the experience of hearing a clock have stopped responding. Habituation is a very fundamental property of the nervous system. Virtually any response will eventually diminish if the precipitating stimulus is presented a sufficient number of times. Research conducted by behaviour therapists suggested that habituation could also explain why anxiety diminished during exposure exercises. The nervous system was simply getting bored of the feared object, and ceasing to generate the physical and mental state recognized as anxiety.

Although 'flooding' proved to be an effective treatment for anxiety problems, few behaviour therapists chose to employ it on a routine basis. Instead, a modified form of systematic desensitization became standard practice. Several elements of Wolpe's original procedure were retained, while others were omitted. Patients were still encouraged to confront distressing situations of increasing difficulty; however, particular emphasis was given to conducting this confrontation in real life, rather than in imagination. Relaxation was no longer considered a necessary part of the treatment procedure. This approach is now usually described as *graded exposure*. Although relaxation was no longer used in the treatment of phobias, it was found to have other uses, most notably as a treatment for *insomnia* and *tension headaches*. Thus, behaviour therapy began to be used for problems commonly encountered in general practice rather than in psychiatric settings.

The success of exposure-based methods of treatment in cases of anxiety inspired therapists to revise their approach to many problems that, at least in part, were attributable to anxiety. Even practitioners who were not, strictly speaking, part of the behavioural tradition adopted treatment strategies in which 'exposure' and the provision of clear instructions were key ingredients. A good example of this was the development of *sex therapy* in the 1970s. William Masters and Virginia Johnson developed a framework within which a number of sexual problems could be treated. Their two-week programme attempted to eliminate anxiety related to *performance expectations*. Such expectations were thought to lie at the root of many sexual problems, such as an inability to achieve an erection in men, or an inability to enjoy penetrative sex in women.

Masters and Johnson asked their patients to take part in what they described as a *sensate focus* programme. This was, in many respects, simply graded exposure to the sexual situation. Couples were forbidden to attempt intercourse until they had undertaken a series of exercises in which the amount of erotic contact was slowly increased. Only when both participants felt comfortable in the sexual situation could intercourse be attempted. Eventually, the basic sensate focus programme was supplemented by more specific exercises for specific problems. For example, a woman who was unable to achieve orgasm might benefit from strengthening the muscle groups responsible for orgasmic sensations. This could be achieved by practising some simple physical exercises (such as stopping and starting the flow of urine when emptying the bladder). Again, to the amazement of those practising in the psychoanalytic tradition, these straightforward strategies proved remarkably effective.

In 1960, systematic desensitization and the bed-pad and alarm were the only representatives of the new field of behaviour therapy. Understandably, academic journals carried virtually no articles on work being conducted by what was then only a few practitioners; however, by 1970, nearly a thousand articles on behaviour therapy were being published every year. Moreover, by the 1970s the characteristics of behaviour therapy were becoming clearer. This new approach was the virtual antithesis of psychoanalysis. Therapy was brief, lasting weeks or months rather than years, and the relationship between therapist and patient was not considered to play an important part in process of change. Although fears and phobias might have their roots in the past (due to prior conditioning), behaviour therapists expressed little interest in their actual origins. It was considered more important to know how to treat a problem than to understand why it had developed. Thus, behaviour therapists were very active during sessions, providing patients with instructions, techniques, and in some cases, equipment (for example, the bed-pad and alarm). Moreover, there was a strong emphasis on self-help; patients were encouraged to undertake homework assignments (such as graded exposure exercises or sensate focus). Many critical psychoanalysts suggested that behaviour therapists were merely dealing with symptoms, rather than addressing causes; however, few patients suffered from *symptom substitution*, the replacement of one symptom by another due to neglect of causal factors. Within a decade, behaviour therapy had become established as the most effective treatment for anxiety problems. Yet its successes were not celebrated in the media. In fact, behaviour therapy seemed to make people uneasy.

There had always been something in the cast of behaviourism that disconcerted those with political sensitivities. Watson's manifesto had stressed prediction and control. All science is of course about prediction, but somehow the equal emphasis on control was viewed with suspicion. This general unease about the philosophical foundations of behaviourism came sharply into focus when operant conditioning techniques were employed to 'control' patients with profound behavioural and emotional problems. The method became known as the token economy. In 1961, two psychologists, T. Ayllon and N. H. Azrin, were given a ward of chronically ill psychiatric patients to manage according to behavioural principles. Patients received rewards when they spontaneously performed desirable behaviours, such as bed making or hair combing; however, rewards were withdrawn when they exhibited any of their 'symptoms', such as shouting or offending other patients. The rewards took the form of *plastic tokens* that could be collected and exchanged for privileges, such as listening to records, going to see films or obtaining extra food. The ward had, in effect, been turned into a giant Skinner box. Desirable behaviours were reinforced, and undesirable behaviours were punished. Patients were subjected to the same type of reinforcement schedule that enabled Skinner to teach his pigeons to play ping-pong.

The token economy was very successful. The work of Ayllon and Azrin was replicated in other institutions, proving that even the most florid symptoms of chronic mental illness could be extinguished. Patients with schizophrenia, who had previously screamed, hurled abuse and buried their faces in their food, became docile. Incontinent patients acquired bladder control and mute patients began to speak. So successful were many of these token economy programmes that patients who had been confined for decades were, quite suddenly, given their freedom. Here then was a situation that had curious historical resonances. Not since the time of Pinel had those condemned to a life of suffering outside the reach of medicine and compassion been offered such a reprieve. Yet this twentieth-century liberation of La Bicêtre received few plaudits. The token economy seemed to militate against the prevailing view of what a human being should be. Freud had suggested that man was nothing more than a beast. Behaviourism went further. Man was less than a beast. He was a machine. And worse of all, for the liberal left, a machine that operated on capitalist principles!

In addition to the token economy, a further treatment aroused doubts as to the propriety of the behavioural approach. This was *aversion therapy*, a rather jarring combination of words reminiscent of the slogans featured in George Orwell's *1984*. In Orwell's depressing vision of an England under totalitarian rule, citizens learn to accept that 'War is Peace' and 'Freedom is Slavery'. Aversion therapy was a method of treatment devised to change the mind through repetitive punishment. Typically, aversion therapy was used to 'extinguish' sexual interest in objects or persons deemed by society to be deviant. Such 'perverse' interests were thought to be the result of a faulty 'learning history', and thus, a legitimate target for 'unlearning'. In the standard treatment procedure of this kind, a homosexual might be shown homoerotic images paired with an electric shock. Termination of the shock was then associated with the presentation of a heterosexual erotic image. Thus, using a Skinnerian vocabulary, homosexual feelings were 'punished', while 'negative reinforcement' was employed to encourage heterosexual feelings.

Remarkably, behaviour therapists seemed to pay scant regard to the ethical issues such work raised. Who decides what is to be conditioned 'into' or 'out of' an individual's mind? Is homosexuality an illness, or is it merely a preference? If homosexuality is not an illness, why should it be treated? Even if an individual claimed that he or she were unhappy being homosexual, is that really the individual's problem, or does the fault lie within society? These, and other related questions, were simply set aside. Of course, psychoanalysts had been equally guilty of describing certain sexual preferences as examples of mental illness; however, their method of treatment did not recollect images of the torture chamber. With the advent of aversion therapy, it was as though the stocks and manacles of the old bedlam had been revived in a modern guise. Worse still, aversion therapy was nowhere near as effective as other behavioural treatments. The critics were not amused.

Flooding, the token economy and aversion therapy were all received, to a greater or lesser extent, with considerable suspicion. Even sex therapy became associated with adverse tabloid-style publicity. The successes of behaviour therapy were consistently under-reported, while the more dubious treatment procedures were given sensational coverage; however, in retrospect, it is clear that techniques such as the token economy and aversion therapy had simply focused an already widespread negative attitude to behavioural psychology per se. Even when behaviourism was still in the gestation phase, many influential commentators took exception to its philosophical foundations. In *Everybody's Political What's What*, the writer and playwright, George Bernard Shaw, said of Pavlov's work: 'it denies . . . any metaphysical factors in life whatsoever, including purpose, intuition, inspiration, and all the religious and artistic impulses. It boycotts volition, conscience . . . In short, it seeks to abolish life and mind.' Shaw's grim judgement has continued to reverberate through the twentieth century, providing a firm foundation for aspirant anti-behavioural polemicists.

Human beings regard their actions as the direct result of intention. One action is purposely chosen in preference to another. If Pavlov's work challenged this supposition, then his ideological heir, Skinner, rejected it entirely. The latter suggested that mental states are not the cause of behaviour at all. Rather, the entire repertoire of human action is made more or less likely by experience of past consequences. Human beings simply think that their behaviour is intentional. In fact, it is just a product of prior learning. Some behaviours are reinforced, and are therefore retained, while others are punished, and subsequently extinguished.

Skinner's rigid adherence to a mechanistic view of humanity served only to strengthen existing anti-behavioural prejudices. Yet Skinner himself found this concept curiously uplifting. Indeed, he found the idea of 'man as machine' so inspiring that he promptly wrote a Utopian novel, *Walden Two*, in which he describes an ideal society. In it, behavioural principles are employed as a means of maintaining perfect social control. *Walden Two* was published in 1948, the year that Orwell reversed the last two digits for the virtually simultaneous publication of *1984*.

In Orwell's *1984*, and its predecessor, Aldous Huxley's *Brave New World* published in 1932, two quite different dystopian worlds are prophesied; however, both are linked by a 'behavioural' conception of humanity. Like Orwell, Huxley's vision is set in England, though some six hundred years in the future. In both works, conditioning principles are employed to deprive the individual of free will. It is often said that, in classical music, composers always give the devil the best tunes. In the history of behavioural psychology, dystopians have always spoken more eloquently. *Walden Two*, Skinner's behavioural Utopia, pales into insignificance when compared with *1984* and *Brave New World*. However, the behavioural cause was finally sunk, in literature at least, with the publication of Anthony Burgess' *A Clockwork Orange* in 1962, a coruscating attack on behaviourism, and a work of shocking prescience that actually predicted the arrival of aversion therapy several years in advance.

In *A Clockwork Orange*, Alex, a delinquent whose only interests are rape, 'ultra violence' and classical music, is offered a reduced prison sentence if he agrees to undergo a conditioning treatment called Ludovico's technique. He is shown images of appalling violence in a drug-induced state of nausea. After the treatment, the mere thought of violence produces weakness and vomiting. Unfortunately, he is also unable to listen to classical music without exhibiting a similar response. Beethoven's fifth symphony was used to accompany the violent images shown during conditioning and his 'conditioned disgust' has generalized to all forms of music that move him. Alex is robbed of his free will, and the reader is forced to ask: who is the greater threat to civilized society, the delinquent, or the Pavlovian therapists who deprive him of his ability to make choices? Before the real behaviour therapists had progressed very far with their first treatment programmes for 'sexual deviance', aversion therapy had been damned.

Yet behaviourism, for all its faults, has been condemned out of context. Few critics ever pause to consider what ideas behaviourism opposed in the first half of the twentieth century. Psychoanalytic thinking is taken to be the traditional enemy, but behaviourism had a far more fundamental battle on its hands. The battle was fought against eugenics, that is, the belief that human development is predetermined by genes and therefore largely unaffected by the influence of learning and experience. When Watson was writing his manifesto, *prediction and control* did not have the ominous connotations they have now. These words suggested that human development could be, as it were, cultivated. Human nature was, according to Watson, malleable.

In fiction, behavioural dystopias take the erosion of choice as their principal theme; however, in Watson's time, behaviourism was, ironically, all about choice. Each child is born with unlimited potential. The hope and optimism of Watson's outlook is captured in a famous quote, in which he promises a genuinely brave new world: 'Give me a dozen healthy infants, well-formed, and my own specified world to bring them up in and I'll guarantee to take any one at random and train him to become any type of specialist I might select – doctor, lawyer, merchant-chief and yes, even beggar-man and thief, regardless of his talents, penchants, tendencies, abilities, vocations, and race of his ancestors.' For Watson, ancestry meant nothing. For eugenists, on the other hand, ancestry was everything.

Darwin's evolutionary doctrine had an immediate impact on the thinking of his day; moreover, a particular inference derived from Darwinian theory caused considerable alarm. If man had evolved from the ape, then surely it must also be possible to degenerate back again. Indeed, Darwin himself was concerned about the moderating consequences of modern living on the process of natural selection, and by implication, the effect of this on the human race. The biologist Alfred Wallace recalled a conversation with Darwin in 1880: 'In one of my last conversations with Darwin he expressed himself very gloomily on the future of humanity, on the ground that in our modern civilization natural selection had no play, and the fittest did not survive . . . and it is notorious that our population is more largely renewed in each generation from the lower than from the middle and upper classes.'

Even before Darwin had formalized his ideas on evolution, it was well known that by careful selection farmers and horticulturalists could enhance particular characteristics. Francis Galton, a cousin of Darwin, believed that the same careful selection could be employed with respect to man. Indeed, the application of breeding principles to the human race might afford some protection against the threat of degeneration. It is difficult to date the beginning of Galton's new science of eugenics; however, he was expressing eugenic ideas as early as 1865. In a two-part article for *Macmillan's Magazine*, Galton suggested that the state should establish who in society had hereditary merit, and celebrate such individuals in public ceremonies. The elite should be encouraged to marry in Westminster Abbey, and postnatal grants should be provided to encourage fecundity. The less worthy might be segregated, and prevented from procreating. Within thirty years, eugenic ideas were being taken very seriously indeed. By 1903, the British parliament had established a commission on 'national deterioration'. The National Eugenics Education Society was formed in 1907 and the American Eugenics Society in 1923. Eugenists originally saw the signs of evolutionary decline in the 'feeble-minded'; however, in a very short time the mentally ill, prostitutes and the unemployed were all considered a danger to the *germ plasm*.

In some of the more rabid works of the late nineteenth century, certain types of art were thought to show the marks of degeneration. The finest example of this genre of paranoid writing is *Degeneration*, published by the Hungarian physician Max Nordau in 1895. He saw the signs of degeneration everywhere: in the caste of an individual's face and in the fashion of the day. In the contemporary concert hall he heard only the howling of beasts, and as for impressionist art, surely the fragmentation and distortion represented nothing more than the product of an enfeebled nervous system. To read Nordau is to read the script of a 1950s science fiction B-movie: 'There is a sound of rending in every tradition, and it is as though the morrow would not link itself with today. Things as they are totter and plunge, and they are suffered to reel and fall . . .' Something terrible was about to happen. How his dreams would have been disturbed by apocalyptic visions. In the ruins of the Sorbonne, perhaps, half men lifting books from the rubble. The sky lit by fires in the capitals of Europe, as culture burned . . . In the climate of the post-Darwinian nightmare the eugenics movement flourished. Eugenic programmes, often initiated under the banner of *race hygiene*, soon developed in Sweden, Norway, Russia, Switzerland, Poland, France and Italy. In the 1920s, the eugenic creed spread to Latin America and Japan. Needless to say, right-wing thinkers in Germany had also warmed to the idea.

In Britain, Home Secretary Winston Churchill privately expressed to Prime Minister Herbert Asquith that the proliferation of the mentally deficient was a 'very terrible danger to the race'. In May 1912, the government introduced the Mental Deficiency Bill, which allowed the detention and segregation of the 'feeble-minded'. Eventually, gender segregation would stop the feeble-minded from procreating altogether. In America, a more proactive approach was endorsed: sterilization. By the end of the 1920s sterilization was accepted in 24 states. By the mid-1930s, over twenty thousand sterilizations had been legally performed in the United States; there is of course no record of informal sterilizations. Although these programmes were designed to restrict the reproductive success of those we would now describe as learning disabled, numerous 'wayward women' were also sterilized. In retrospect, it is likely that many of these women were poorly educated, unhappy or simply independent! In 1934, sterilization laws became effective in Germany. Within three years, the authorities had sterilized 225,000 people. This prompted a prominent American eugenist in Virginia to accelerate the state sterilization programme. His words now resonate with profound irony: 'The Germans are beating us at our own game'. The eugenic movement came to an abrupt and timely end when the full horror of the Nazi biomedical vision was realized. In the wake of the holocaust, it was difficult to justify a eugenic philosophy. Behavioural dystopias are, on the whole, only to be found in works of fiction. Eugenic dystopias are described in our history books.

CHAPTER 5

The Search for Meaning

'Some forms of death are easier than others: death takes on qualities which differ according to each man's way of thinking.'

Michel de Montaigne, *On Vanity*

Prisoner 119104 arrived at the camp on a crowded transportation train just before the dawn. He and his fellow occupants were greeted by an SS officer who directed the vast majority of passengers to the left and a few others to the right. 119104 had been asked to stand with the smaller group. At the time, he had thought nothing of this; he had noted only the officer's spotless uniform and his manner of careless ease, pointing with his forefinger this way, then that.

When evening came, 119104 joined a band of seasoned prisoners and asked one of them about the possible whereabouts of a friend. A friend who had been with him on the train, but who, on arrival, had been directed to the left, instead of to the right. The man gestured towards a chimney a few hundred yards off. It was sending a column of flame into the sky and disgorged clouds of acrid smoke. 'That's where your friend is', said the veteran prisoner, 'floating up to heaven.' This was the first of many losses that 119104 would suffer in Auschwitz. By 1945, his beloved wife, his brother and both his parents would also be sent to the crematoria or simply perish in the death camps.

During the unforgiving winter of 1944, 119104 was ordered to dig a tunnel. The Polish soil was frozen solid; however, he had become accustomed to a punishing regimen of interminable hard labour. Sometimes he was reduced to a near stuporous state of exhaustion. When the tunnel was completed, he was rewarded with some coupons. They were worth 12 cigarettes. Within the black market of the camp, 12 cigarettes could be exchanged for 12 soups, and for 119104, 12 soups was the difference between life and death.

Curiously, the relentless and uncompromising camp regimen failed to break habits that 119104 had established over a lifetime. One of these was his continuous – almost involuntary – observation of human behaviour. He had noticed that some prisoners had a greater will to live than others. There were those who, even when in possession of cigarettes, would choose to smoke them, starve and die. For such individuals, the gas chamber was a mere formality. They had stopped living long before they were given a bar of soap and ushered into the 'bath house'. 119104 began to wonder if there was a common factor that distinguished prisoners who struggled to survive from those who gave up. He made some notes on scraps of paper and began to develop a theory that might account for the differences that he observed.

When the Second World War ended, 119104 was able to resume his existence as Viktor Frankl, an Austrian psychiatrist. He had lost everything he valued. With the exception of his sister, his entire family had been killed. Yet he emerged from the holocaust with a profound understanding of human suffering. His observations, particularly regarding the character of survivors, became the foundation of a new approach to psychotherapy. Thirteen years after the liberation of Auschwitz, he collected his ideas together in a book that took him only nine days to write. It was published in 1959 and entitled *From Death Camp to Existentialism*. The book was subsequently updated and later republished as *Man's Search for Meaning*, under which title it is better known.

Frankl had been given the dubious privilege of witnessing the effects of extreme stress on the mind. Yet his conclusions about the causes of suffering show an unexpected depreciation of the role played by stress. For Frankl, events alone – no matter how terrible – are not sufficient to cause suffering. Rather, it is the meaning that an individual attaches to events that will determine whether he or she experiences hope or despair.

Frankl recognized that he had managed to survive for three years in a death camp largely because of good fortune. On the morning of his arrival at Auschwitz, the well-groomed SS officer might just as easily have directed him to the left, as to the right; however, Frankl did not attribute his survival solely to the fickle sway of blind chance. On the contrary, he believed that he had survived by distinguishing his suffering with meaning.

During his years in Auschwitz, Frankl had discovered that his determination to find purpose in his own life and suffering was reflected in the character of fellow survivors. Those individuals who refused to give up were also those who possessed what he described as a *will to meaning*. Summarizing his position, Frankl suggests that 'everything can be taken from a man but one thing: the last of the human freedoms – to choose one's attitude in any given circumstances . . .'

Even though he and his fellow prisoners were under constant threat of death, bereft of every possession, hungry, cold and bereaved, they were still capable of choosing to experience emotions such as joy, particularly when inspired by natural beauty. In *Man's Search for Meaning*, Frankl underscores this point by describing the events of one evening, when a man rushed into his hut and urged everyone present to go outside in order to enjoy the sunset: 'Standing outside we saw . . . the whole sky alive with clouds of ever-changing shapes and colours, from steel blue to blood red. The desolate grey mud huts provided a sharp contrast, while the puddles on the muddy ground reflected the glowing sky. Then, after minutes of moving silence, one prisoner said to another, "How beautiful the world could be!"'

Concentration camp prisoners who have abandoned hope and psychiatric patients may appear to occupy very different worlds; however, Frankl was of the opinion that they were alike in one very important respect. The suffering of both groups shared a common cause: a failure to find *meaning* in life. Frankl coined a new term, the *noogenic neuroses*, to describe the kind of difficulties that develop when the 'will to meaning' is frustrated. Later, he developed a therapeutic approach to complement his theoretical ideas. He called this approach logotherapy, from the Greek *logos*, translatable as meaning.

In logotherapy, the therapist accepts the subjective experience of the patient without question. The therapist does not endorse the notion that suffering is a mental 'sickness', and stresses that sadness and fear are simply part of the human condition. An attempt is then made to make sense of the patient's suffering. Frankl was fond of quoting an aphorism of Nietzsche's in order to capture the spirit of his clinical work: 'He who has a why to live for can bear with almost any how.'

Frankl gives a brief but illuminating example of the practice of logotherapy. An elderly general practitioner once consulted him because of a severe depression. The depression had clearly developed after the death of the doctor's wife, two years earlier. Frankl asked him: 'What would have happened, Doctor, if you had died first, and your wife would have had to survive you?' The general practitioner replied that she would have suffered terribly. 'You see, Doctor,' said Frankl, 'such suffering has been spared her, and it was you who have spared her this suffering – to be sure, at the price that now you have to survive and mourn her.' The distraught doctor suddenly became calm, shook Frankl's hand and left without saying a word. His suffering had acquired meaning.

Frankl's work has two major distinguishing features. Firstly, his philosophical stance is fundamentally positive. Irrespective of circumstance, human beings have the capacity to overcome adversity. Secondly, emotional distress is closely linked with attitudes and beliefs. Thus, 'thoughts' – which might also be described as *mental events* – are given a far more central position in human affairs than Freudian drives or Pavlovian reflexes. These two features, a positive philosophical stance and a respect for 'cognition' were characteristic of several schools of therapy that emerged in the wake of the Second World War. These schools are usually referred to as *humanistic* and are collectively described as the third force. The word third is used because these schools were preceded by the psychoanalytic and behavioural movements.

Although Frank's writing is distinctly humanistic in nature, he originally described his approach as existential. The same is also true of Fritz Perls, a German analyst who broke with Freudian orthodoxy to establish *gestalt therapy* in the 1950s. Like

Frankl, his brand of existentialism has none of the gloom associated with Sartre and the mainstream European existential movement. Perls believed that the human animal is innately positive and that psychological problems arise only when that innate goodness is frustrated or denied.

The term 'gestalt' is a German word that can be translated in several ways, such as 'form' or 'shape'; however, the most satisfactory translation is most probably 'whole'. Perls borrowed the term from the gestalt school, a group of psychologists working in Berlin before the Second World War, who shared an interest in understanding mental phenomena such as thought, memory and perception. The branch of academic psychology concerned with basic mental functions and processes is called *cognitive psychology*. The gestalt school were, therefore, cognitive psychologists. They undertook a series of laboratory-based investigations of mental processes, and are now remembered mostly for their pioneering studies of perception. They concluded that human beings perceive the world in a holistic way. For example, a melody will still be recognizable as 'the same tune' even when played in different keys. All the individual notes may be different, but the 'shape' or 'form' of the melody is retained.

Gestalt psychologists described a number of mental properties that guide holistic perception. For example, a circle with a small gap in its circumference is still 'recognized' as a circle. It is not perceived as a curved line, the ends of which do not quite meet. The mind automatically fills in the gap. Gestalt psychologists called this property *closure*.

The closest link between gestalt psychology, as explored in the laboratory, and gestalt therapy is a strong emphasis on *holism*. Perls believed that psychological problems were, at least in part, due to the denial of certain emotions. In gestalt therapy, an attempt is made to make individuals 'whole' by increasing their awareness of unacknowledged feelings. Perls had recognized that the relationship between thought and emotion was a close one. Moreover, he began to explore how using different words to describe the same experience could increase or decrease awareness of emotions.

Perls was particularly interested in how his patients used

words to protect themselves from uncomfortable or unwanted feelings. A patient might say: 'You know how it is, when people are in social situations they can get uptight.' Perls urged his patients to 'own' their feelings by requesting the omission of impersonal words or phrases. The patient might then say: 'I know that when I'm with my friends, I usually feel very tense.' Perls found that when his patients modified their language, favouring more personal and less abstract phrases, they became more aware of their emotional state.

A more specific link between experimental gestalt psychology and gestalt therapy is apparent in Perls' use of the term *unfinished business*. Perls suggested that certain problems, particularly those associated with strong emotions, should always be resolved in a conclusive way. If a problem is not resolved, it will continue to affect and possibly disturb the mind. Thus, a man bullied by his father in childhood might have been robbed of the opportunity to retaliate by his father's early death. In this example, the business of retaliation has been thwarted by circumstance and is therefore termed unfinished. Such an individual might have accumulated a backlog of anger that frequently erupts during everyday exchanges and represents a futile effort to satisfy the anachronistic need to retaliate. In the same way that the mind has a tendency to complete imperfect geometric figures, it is also the case that the mind has a tendency to work towards the 'closure' of emotional problems. The incomplete gestalt of an unmet need will continue to disturb the mind, promoting feelings of unease and dissatisfaction. An important part of gestalt therapy is assisting the patient to resolve any unfinished business.

Perls believed that unresolved emotional problems, originating in the past, could be resolved only by addressing their causes in the present. Thus, in the example given above, the patient might be instructed to imagine his deceased father sitting in front of him on a chair. He would then be encouraged to express feelings such as anger and resentment as though his father was actually present. This procedure provides the patient with an opportunity to vent frustrated feelings and subsequently achieve emotional closure. The *empty chair* technique, as it became known, was one of a range of quite dramatic methods employed by Perls to help patients complete unfinished business. Perhaps the most sensational of these was asking patients to play different roles in a re-enactment of past situations.

Although the links between laboratory-based investigations of perception and gestalt therapy are tenuous, the fact that Perls attempted to forge those links is of great interest. It demonstrates a precocious interest in mental processes, as well as in mental events. The term mental event has already been used to describe thoughts; however, the term can also be used to describe anything that enters the conscious mind, for example, an idea, image or impression. *Mental processes*, on the other hand, are those fundamental mechanisms in the mind that, for example, retrieve memories into awareness or guide our attention towards one feature of the environment rather than another.

Perls was showing an interest in cognition at two levels. He was interested not only in 'what' people think, but also in 'how' they think. Moreover, his meticulous attention to language represents an advance on Frankl's view that emotions are determined by attitudes and beliefs. Even the words employed to express a belief may influence the intensity of associated emotions.

Fritz Perls' life was, by any standard, quite extraordinary. His medical training was interrupted by the First World War and from 1916 to 1917 he spent many months living in the trenches. During his term as medical officer for 36 Pioneer Battalion, he was wounded, gassed and eventually decorated for bravery. During the Second World War, Perls joined the South African Army, in which he served as a psychiatrist. In 1946, he settled in America, and began to refine his ideas on therapy and the mind. Over the subsequent two decades, Perls' reputation grew; however, he reached the apogee of his fame during his term as a resident trainer at the Esalen Institute, Big Sur, California. The Institute, with its panoramic views over the Pacific Ocean, was everything that a progressive centre for the study of human potential should be. During the 1960s it became a mecca for liberal free-thinkers. Indeed, its influence was so extensive that it was featured in a best-selling novel and parodied in a famous film called *Bob and Carol and Ted and Alice*.

Perls seized the moment and transformed himself into one of the quintessential emblems of the 1960s: the guru. The trappings of bourgeois respectability were swiftly disavowed, to be replaced by beads, sandals, a flowing robe and a long white beard. Perhaps, under the influence of voguish eastern philosophy, he composed a gestalt prayer, which begins with the now embarrassing lines: 'I do my thing, and you do your thing.' It is ironic that gestalt therapy chooses holism and integration as its principal themes. It seems implausible, that the 23-year-old trench soldier and the 76-year-old guru could have looked across the landscape of Perls' psyche and recognized each other as the same man.

Typically, Perls trod the grandiose path to oblivion shared by many icons of the 1960s. He declared himself the world's greatest therapist and proclaimed that he was also a hero in the history of modern science. He suggested that gestalt therapy was the only realistic and effective way of stopping both civil and nuclear war, and in keeping with the lax morality of the time, openly admitted to having affairs with patients. The great tragedy of Fritz Perls is that he allowed his ego to eclipse his contribution to psychotherapy. On account of his personal excesses, gestalt therapy has become associated with outlandish ideas and the abuse of patients. This is unfortunate, because Perls' recognition that experimental cognitive psychology and psychotherapy might enjoy a fruitful collaboration was a display of astonishing prescience.

Although Frankl and Perls are humanistic in outlook, the term *humanistic psychotherapy* has become more strongly associated with the psychologist Carl Rogers than any other single individual. He was born in 1902 and raised in the mid-west of the United States. Both of Rogers' parents were Christian fundamentalists and displayed characteristic enthusiasm for traditional values. Although Rogers' father was a successful businessman, he purchased a farm in order to remove his family from the temptations of suburban life. Even so, young Carl could not be entirely protected from the sinful commerce of the world, and he would later write: 'I remember my slight feeling of wickedness when I had my first bottle of "pop".' Here then was a very different figure to Frankl or Perls.

Rogers' education began in the shadow of his parents' expectations. He attended the Union Theological Seminary, New York to 'prepare for religious work'; however, he left after only two years and moved to Teachers College, Columbia University, also in New York. While at Teachers College, he became interested in clinical psychology and subsequently spent 12 years working in a child guidance clinic. From 1945 to 1957 he was professor of psychology at the University of Chicago, and it was during this time that he refined and developed non-directive or *client-centred therapy*.

Irrespective of Rogers' subsequent rejection of the religious beliefs of his parents, their influence on his personal development is undeniable. His writings are saturated with a sense of decency and wholesomeness – an agrarian, god-fearing simplicity that has more in common with Aaron Copland's *Appalachian Spring* than the writings of Freud or Breuer. Indeed, the appearance of Carl Rogers in a poem by Robert Frost would hardly arouse concern. Unfortunately, Rogers' folksy image has been a serious obstacle to the proper appreciation of client-centred therapy. His ideas about the importance of forming a genuine and warm relationship with the patient are routinely given precedence over his more technical contributions, for example, his views on the mental processes that govern the operation of defence mechanisms.

In the hands of Carl Rogers, the torch of humanistic optimism is carried to new heights, where it burns with fierce intensity. According to Rogers, 'One of the most revolutionary concepts to grow out of our clinical experience is the growing recognition that the innermost core of man's nature, the deepest layers of his personality, the base of his "animal nature" is positive in nature – is basically socialized, forward-moving, rational and realistic'. It is difficult to imagine a sharper contrast with the Freudian view of man's *core nature*: selfish, backward-looking, impulsive and 'fantastic'. Freudian and humanistic conceptions of humanity are in total opposition.

Rogers believed that the natural inclination of humankind, towards the good and positive, was attributable to what he described as the *self-actualizing tendency*. The term self-actualization was originally used by Jung; however, when used by humanistic psychologists it has a different, and arguably more precise, meaning. In Rogers' scheme, the self-actualizing tendency is perhaps best considered a drive that motivates the individual to maximize his or her potential in all areas. According to Rogers, all psychological problems arise when the self-actualizing tendency is blocked or frustrated.

In client-centred therapy, identity problems are given special emphasis with respect to the formation of symptoms. Rogers made a useful distinction between the *self* and the *self-concept*. The self is an individual's true self. It is the identity referred to in sayings such as 'To thine own self be true'. The self is a collection of dispositions and preferences that represent personality at its most fundamental level. The self-concept, on the other hand, is an individual's perception of self, who the individual thinks he or she is. Rogers makes this distinction because the self and self-concept can be discrepant. When self and self-concept overlap, the individual is said to be in a *congruent state*. Such an individual experiences few, if any, psychological symptoms; however, if the correspondence between self and self-concept is poor, then the individual is said to be in an *incongruent state*, and is likely to experience inner tension, discomfort and dissatisfaction. The greater the disparity between self and self-concept, the more intense these psychological symptoms will become.

Rogers believed that the development of the self-concept is determined by external factors, most notably the expectations of others. A typical example of an 'incongruent' individual might be a young man, born with artistic gifts, but raised in a house in which science-based professions are highly valued. He might be urged to study sciences and ultimately qualify as a doctor, yet achieve little job satisfaction. In Rogerian terms, his self-actualizing tendency has been blocked or frustrated. By forming a concept of self based on the expectations of others, and living his life according to the aspirations of a 'false self', his true needs have not been met.

The self-concept develops from – and is guided by – a set of acquired and deep-seated beliefs. Rogers suggested that all infants are born into the world with a need for *positive regard*, that is, the approval and love of others. As infants grow in a social environment, it is inevitable that some behaviours, but not others, will meet with approval. The infant begins to develop what Rogers called *conditions of worth*. These beliefs may have their origins in infancy; however, they often persist into adulthood. Moreover, they may become more sophisticated, corresponding with escalating demands and expectations. A simple example of a condition of worth might be: 'Achievement is important and I am less of a person if I do not achieve.' It is easy to see how such a belief might have been cultivated within a competitive family is which approval was wholly dependent on academic success. The most important feature of 'conditions of worth' is that they do not reflect the values of an individual's true self. In seeking to behave in a way that is consistent with his or her conditions of worth, the individual constantly risks frustrating the self-actualizing tendency. The discrepancy between self and self-concept widens, and the individual experiences increasing levels of dissatisfaction.

According to Rogers, the self-concept is maintained by defence mechanisms. When an individual begins to realise that there is a discrepancy between the self and self-concept, this causes considerable discomfort. Thoughts such as 'I'm wasting my life' or 'I don't want to go on like this' might enter awareness. To reduce this discomfort, defences such as *distortion* and *denial* come into operation. They usually serve to reduce the conflict that arises from acknowledging the discrepant aims of the self and self-concept. For example, an individual who has opted for a career in science (because of parental expectations) might be unexpectedly complimented and told that he is creative. By distorting the situation, and concluding that the compliment is insincere, conflict between self and self-concept can be reduced. Similarly, an individual raised to believe that 'sex is wrong' might deny experiencing ordinary sexual feelings. Such an individual will experience sexual arousal; however, he or she will simply fail to acknowledge the meaning and significance of these feelings.

When defensive mechanisms are operating, the quality of

thinking itself suffers. Attitudes may become less flexible, and ideas are sometimes expressed in a simplified form. Crude *overgeneralizations* will make more frequent appearances, for example, 'All art is a waste of time'. Moreover, the individual begins to accept these summary judgements as facts. *Intentional reactions* was the term chosen by Rogers to describe the impoverished, irrational thinking that occurs when defences are operating.

Like Perls, Rogers expressed a keen interest in mental processes. His emphasis on distortion and denial as defences was most probably influenced by laboratory work. During the 1940s and 1950s, laboratory-based studies of human perception were yielding some very interesting results. Essentially, this work showed that perception itself was not a neutral process. The eye is not a camera. Indeed, the eye is rarely faithful. What experimental subjects saw in laboratory tests was very much influenced by their expectations and beliefs. It was as though mental filters were operating in the mind (at an unconscious level) and editing the contents of awareness. Rogers borrowed the concept of *subception* (or *pre-perception*) to explain how defences work. Any information that contradicts or threatens the self-concept might be subject to a preliminary analysis, evaluated as 'dangerous', and either be excluded from awareness or at least be modified before being permitted to enter the conscious mind. Rogers' views on the relationship between subception and defences is a further example of a link made between laboratory-based cognitive psychology and clinical practice.

Many of Rogers' ideas are derived from Freud. Conflict within the person causes anxiety, and defences come into operation to reduce that anxiety. The cost of defensiveness is to lose touch with reality. However, Rogers shows much more concern with detail. He describes the type of beliefs that have the potential to divide the ego, speculates on the processes that must be involved in the operation of defence mechanisms, and yet more importantly, considers how these factors influence the quality of thought. Rogers was a very 'cognitive' clinical psychologist. Indeed, his approach is consistent with fellow humanist Abraham Maslow, who once observed that the neurotic is not *emotionally sick*, but *cognitively wrong*.

In spite of the technical nature of his formulation, Rogers' client-centred therapy is surprisingly straightforward. In therapy, Rogers suggested that the patient – or his preferred term client – be given *unconditional positive regard.* The patient is thus offered a 'no strings attached' relationship. Rogers believed that healthy individuals are those raised by parents capable of prizing their children, even though they might not value equally everything the child does or says. Therefore, the client-centred therapist attempts to be completely non-judgemental and exudes empathy. Rogers went to some lengths in his writings to stress the importance of the therapist's personal qualities, most notably warmth and sincerity. Rogerian therapy is explicitly, therefore, a kind of re-parenting.

The client-centred therapist never offers interpretations or advice. Instead, he or she simply paraphrases and confirms the patient's disclosures. This process of *reflecting* statements back to the patient shows that the therapist is listening carefully. There is a tacit communication to the patient that he or she is worth listening to, and subsequently this process is thought to strengthen the patient's sense of self-worth. In addition, the therapist is holding up a mirror, allowing the individual to appreciate more fully his or her emotional state. Thus, as in gestalt therapy, the patient is able to get in touch with unacknowledged feelings.

Eventually, the discrepancies between self and self-concept are diminished, and greater congruency is established between values, beliefs and behaviour. In the absence of conflict, there is no longer a need to mobilize defences, and denial and distortion are replaced by *realistic perception.* Rogers describes this new state as *openness to experience.* The defective thinking that characterizes intentional reactions disappears, to be superseded by a more *rational* approach to life and its problems.

Frankl, Perls and Rogers all shared an interest in understanding the patient's belief system, the relatively fixed set of attitudes that influences an individual's general outlook. A slightly idiosyncratic, yet highly original extension of this interest is found in the work of George Kelly, the founder of *personal construct psychology* (PCP).

Kelly worked for the US navy during the Second World War, and after being discharged, was appointed professor and director of clinical psychology at Ohio State University. In 1955, he published a two-volume work entitled *The Psychology of Personal Constructs*. This was to be his definitive statement, at once a treatise on human nature and a manual for therapists.

PCP is built on a fundamental philosophical idea which Kelly called *constructive alternativism*. In many ways, his stance is similar to that of Viktor Frankl. Human beings can make choices about how they perceive and interpret experiences. Moreover, there are always alternatives from which to choose. Again, the optimism so characteristic of the humanistic school is readily apparent in his writings: 'No one needs paint himself into a corner; no one needs to be completely hemmed in by circumstances; no one needs to be the victim of his biography.' A mind can always be changed.

Kelly subscribed to the view that human beings are fundamentally rational. Indeed, he suggested that people behave like scientists. They develop theories about themselves and the world in which they live. Specific hypotheses are then tested by conducting experiments. Finally, outcomes are observed to establish whether a given theory is correct or incorrect. Behaviour is not the product of habit or a learned reflex, but a tool. Indeed, Kelly described behaviour as 'man's principal instrument of enquiry'.

A particular word, *construing*, was used by Kelly to describe the process of predicting and thereby making sense of one's self and the world. Such predictions are based on *constructs*. Kelly's use of the word construct is idiosyncratic and he invested it with special meaning. A construct is not equivalent to a concept or idea. It is a fundamental unit of understanding. Moreover, it has a very distinctive feature, dichotomy. Thus, 'good' cannot be understood in the absence of 'bad'. 'Up' can only be meaningful if there is 'down'. Therefore, each construct must have two opposite poles. Every human being has a unique 'construct system', or group of constructs, which will guide construing. Moreover, particular things or people are understood according to the degree by which one pole is emphasized in favour of its opposite. Thus, a car enthusiast might judge a Ferrari in terms of 'Good–Bad', 'Fast–Slow' and 'Beautiful–Ugly', with a strong emphasis on the former pole rather than the latter in each construct.

Kelly developed a special method to expose an individual's constructs using what he called the *repertory grid*. A therapist might be interested in how a patient construes work associates. First, the patient is asked to name about ten people at work. These should be varied, reflecting several permutations of relationship. Thus, those who are liked and disliked, superiors and subordinates, men and women, might all be included to ensure a broad and representative sample. The patient is then asked if there is any important way in which any two people are different from a third. The patient might reply that his manager and his assistant are aggressive, whereas his secretary is not. This would suggest the presence of a basic construct, one pole of which might be termed aggressive and the other of which might be termed non-aggressive or passive. The procedure is then repeated using different combinations of work associates to elicit further constructs. Eventually, the therapist is able to identify the principal constructs that determine the patient's attitudes and behaviour with respect to people at work.

It is possible to use the repertory grid technique to elicit constructs relating to any area of life. Usually, the 'elements' are chosen with particular questions in mind. If the issue under discussion is self-identity, then a grid might be devised using elements such as 'me now', 'me in ten years' time', and 'me as I would like to be'. Such a grid might produce constructs such as 'Happy–Sad', 'Successful–Unsuccessful' and 'Employed–Unemployed'.

According to Kelly, negative emotions occur when an individual becomes aware of inadequacies in the construing of events. For example, anxiety might occur under circumstances where events are difficult to interpret or predict. Thus, anxiety is something of an inevitability in entirely new situations, or when something very unexpected happens; however, within Kelly's system, anxiety is also intimately associated with the idea of threat. An individual is threatened when he or she realizes that a change must occur with respect to a core or several core constructs, that is, those constructs associated with the ideas of 'I' or 'Me'. The more fundamental the construct is that must be changed by an event, the more anxious the individual will feel. A very fundamental construct is, of course, 'Alive–Dead', with self-definition tending to emphasize the former. If an event suggests a shift to the latter, this will of course create extreme anxiety.

A distinction has already been made between cognitive events and cognitive processes; however, Kelly's construct system represents an altogether more permanent and deeper feature of the mind. Mental processes will result in the occurrence of mental events, however, both processes and events are by their very nature transitory phenomena. Kelly's constructs might be compared to structures in the mind, a network of values that have the power to influence the formation of attitudes and beliefs, and subsequently affect behaviour.

The concept of *mental structures* had been introduced into psychology many years before Kelly, perhaps most notably by Sir Frederic Bartlett, who in 1932 published a landmark book entitled *Remembering*. It remains one of the classic studies of human memory. In Bartlett's best-known experiment, English people were asked to read an American-Indian folk tale entitled 'War of the Ghosts'. Subsequently, they made repeated efforts to recall what they had previously read. Bartlett noticed that the content and the style of remembered material became progressively distorted with each successive recollection. Moreover, mistakes seemed to reflect a systematic drift away from the foreign narrative of the North American Indians towards the conventions of a traditional English yarn. Bartlett called this phenomenon *rationalization*. For example, in the original tale, 'something black' comes out of the mouth of a dying Indian. English people tended to gradually transform this into the dying Indian foaming at the mouth.

It seemed to Bartlett that his English experimental subjects had, deep in their minds, a set of assumptions about the world which acted as a kind of template. Therefore, any ambiguous or unusual information was being systematically distorted so as to make it fit with the pre-existing world-view. Bartlett called these templates *schemas* or *schemata*.

Schemas have several purposes; however, the most important of these is to help the individual to quickly understand complex information. In Bartlett's experiment, incomprehensible events were made comprehensible by being pressed into the mould of an Englishman's mind. Since Bartlett's time, the existence of schemas has been widely accepted among cognitive psychologists. Schemas are thought to exert a constant influence on perception, judgement and memory, accelerating comprehension and helping the individual to resolve ambiguities. Even the most trivial behaviour, such as shopping, would become exceedingly difficult without the covert operation of relevant schemas.

The schema for the verb 'to buy' will have the common elements of all buying situations. In such situations there is always a vendor, a purchaser, a medium of exchange and some merchandise. The schema for 'to buy' consists of these common elements, although the exact identity of the vendor and purchaser will not be specified, nor the medium of exchange (for example, cash or credit card), nor the object purchased. Because of the existence of a 'to buy' schema, individuals do not have to relearn how to purchase every time a new item is required from a shop. The basic plan or script is simply revived and the detail filled in for each occasion. This is, of course, very much more efficient than relearning what to do on every shopping excursion.

The influence of schemas on understanding and perception was demonstrated in a simple study conducted by two psychologists, J. D. Bransford and M. K. Johnson, in 1972. They presented the following passage to their experimental subjects. It is written in a purposely obscure style: 'The procedure is actually quite simple. First you arrange items into different groups. Of course one pile may be sufficient depending on how much there is to do. If you have to go somewhere else due to lack of facilities that is the next step; otherwise, you are pretty well set. It is important not to overdo things. That is, it is better to do too few things at once than too many . . .' The passage continues in this way until it reaches a similarly baffling conclusion. Individuals who heard the passage untitled regarded it as largely incomprehensible and could remember very little of what was written; however, those who were previously given the title 'Washing Clothes' found the passage easy to understand and recalled more than twice as much as the other group. Relevant knowledge – which constituted a 'washing clothes' schema – had been brought to mind, and clearly affected both the comprehension of the passage and its subsequent committal to memory.

Mental structures, or schemas, are relatively large, integrated systems of knowledge that influence how we understand the world. They can be simple, or highly complex. They can represent something concrete, such as a table, or an abstract concept, such as justice. In the same way that individuals have 'washing clothes' schemas, they also have 'responding to an authoritarian figure' and 'flirting' schemas. It should be noted that psychologists do not believe that mental structures actually exist in the brain, like anatomical structures; however, the term does imply the existence of permanent or semi-permanent knowledge. Such knowledge will influence both mental events and processes.

Kelly's work is important for two reasons. Firstly, he was perhaps the only psychologist to give mental structures a key position in an account of mental disturbance; and secondly, he made great efforts to understand what these cognitive structures might look like. It could be argued that the 'complex', as described by Freud or Jung, is a mental structure; however, the exact nature of 'complexes' is given scant consideration in the psychoanalytic literature. Today, there are few psychologists who would subscribe to the view that the mind houses an architecture of bipolar constructs as Kelly suggested. Nevertheless, the concept of mental structures has frequently re-emerged in the writings of significant psychotherapists since the Second World War, and Kelly is routinely cited as a major influence.

Although many personal construct therapists view Kelly as a true original, existing outside the humanistic tradition, his optimism, emphasis on rationality, and concern with cognition in its broadest sense, place him very much within its compass; however, Kelly, perhaps more than any other of his contemporaries, has always occupied a rather peripheral position in psychology. This is largely because his writing is extremely dense and his use of obscure jargon can make the text difficult to understand.

A far more accessible approach to psychotherapy can be found in the work of Albert Ellis, a clinical psychologist who originally trained as a psychoanalyst with a member of Karen Horney's circle. He held several hospital and academic posts, but spent most of his time in private practice, working largely with people with sexual problems. Ellis soon became disillusioned with psychoanalytic methods and began to devise techniques of his own. He was much inspired by philosophical writings, most notably Marcus Aurelius, Spinoza and Bertrand Russell; however, he owes a particular debt to the Stoic philosopher Epictetus, who once wrote: 'Men are disturbed not by things, but by the views that they take of them.' Ellis had found that he was able to distil certain principles from these philosophical works, principles that could be used within psychotherapy to good effect. In 1956, he addressed the American Psychological Association and introduced his new approach: *rational emotive therapy* (RET).

RET can be placed in the humanist tradition, insofar as Ellis believed that human beings are, at their most basic, rational. They are capable of making decisions and formulating plans that will help them to pursue personal happiness; however, this rational tendency is easily disrupted, particularly in individuals whose brains are 'predisposed' to develop irrational thinking patterns. When irrational thinking predominates, the individual is likely to experience psychological problems. Although Ellis believed that irrationality could be the result of environmental influences (for example, having superstitious parents), he was convinced that the ultimate source of irrationality was biological. Even so, this did not stop him from advocating psychological methods of treatment.

From earliest times, writers and philosophers have commented on a particular duality with respect to mental life. This is the duality that exists between thinking and feeling. The ancient Greeks were the first to make a distinction between passion and reason, and this distinction has since been preserved and respected within the ambit of western culture.

Shakespeare's characters are torn between 'blood and judgement' in much the same way as Freud's cases suffer because of the opposing demands of id and ego. Ellis was not altogether happy with this sharp distinction. Indeed, he suggested that emotions are determined largely by *self-talk*, that is, what individuals are saying to themselves at any given moment. RET is based on the premise that emotional disorders can be treated by attempting to modify self-talk 'directly'. In most forms of psychotherapy, an attempt is made to change the person in some way, and this fundamental change is considered necessary if their thinking is to change. Ellis, on the other hand, advocated a direct attack on the thinking process itself. If a person is to be changed, then their unhelpful thoughts must be identified and corrected.

Ellis developed a simple theoretical framework within which to discuss the relationship between thoughts and feelings. It is known as the *ABC* framework and can be used to demonstrate how the impact of an event on an individual's emotional state is affected by thinking. In Ellis' system, 'A' stands for the *activating event*, 'B' stands for *beliefs* and 'C' stands for *consequences*. If an individual attends a job interview (the activating event) and experiences rejection, he or she might become aware of several commonplace beliefs. Two examples might be 'I don't like getting rejected' and 'Looks like I'll have difficulty finding another job'. The consequence of thinking in this way might be sorrow or regret; however, it is unlikely that such thinking will cause any serious emotional distress. Indeed, ultimately such thinking may have some desirable effects. An example might be strengthening a resolution to fill in more job application forms or prompting a decision to retrain.

A second individual might have an identical experience of rejection; however, he or she might become aware of a rather different set of beliefs. Examples are 'How awful it is to get rejected' and 'I can't stand rejection; it proves I am an inadequate person'. The consequence of thinking in this way might be severe mood disturbance. Moreover, he or she might then refuse to attend other interviews, thus prolonging unemployment. In the first example, the rejected applicant becomes aware of rational beliefs, whereas in the second the rejected applicant becomes aware of irrational beliefs. Clearly, it is the latter set of beliefs that have the potential to promote depression, anxiety and self-defeating behaviour.

Ellis found that certain irrational beliefs tended to cluster together in patients suffering from psychological problems. Also, these fundamental irrational beliefs appeared to possess certain characteristics. For example, they were often expressed like demands or commands. Ellis' familiarity with the teachings of Karen Horney would, no doubt, have made him sensitive to the language his patients used when talking about their beliefs. Horney had referred to the 'tyranny of shoulds' to describe the means by which the superego wields its influence. Ellis noted that his patients also tended to use phrases like 'I should' or 'I must' with alarming frequency. Indeed, with respect to the latter, he coined the term *must-urbating*. Words like 'should' or 'must', appearing in the context of beliefs, generally reflect very high personal standards. If these standards are unrealistically high, they will almost invariably lead to disappointment and dissatisfaction.

Like Rogers, who it will be recalled described 'intentional reactions', Ellis was aware that irrational thinking was less sophisticated than rational thought. In addition to 'overgeneralization', Ellis described features such as *awfulizing*, which involves constantly appraising events as more catastrophic than they actually are, and *misattribution*, which involves the frequent acceptance of blame for no good reason.

Ellis has more in common with Rogers than a recognition of the characteristics of irrational thought. He was also of an optimistic disposition, and he urged patients in his care to accept themselves 'unconditionally'; however, whereas Rogers believed that irrational thinking would slowly disappear as a consequence of forming a relationship with a non-judgemental therapist, Ellis believed that irrational thinking would not change unless actively disputed. His style, therefore, was perhaps more confrontational than any of his predecessors. It was also clearly influenced by his keen interest in philosophy. In much the same way as the validity of a particular proposition might be tested within the context of a philosophical argument, so it was that Ellis disputed the accuracy of irrational thoughts by engaging his patients in a kind of academic debate. As a result of this process, irrational beliefs were proved invalid, then rejected, to be replaced by more rational beliefs.

In psychoanalysis, the patient is allowed to free-associate, while the therapist listens and offers an occasional interpretation. Ellis represents the complete antithesis of this approach. Every thought is subject to close scrutiny and probed for weaknesses. In Freudian psychology, human suffering stems ultimately from the id, the wellspring of the passions. Under Ellis' jurisdiction, human suffering had become a far more intellectual concept. Paraphrasing Descartes, a patient in Ellis' surgery might proclaim with impunity: 'I think, therefore I suffer.'

By the 1960s, it was possible to take stock of developments in psychotherapy since the Second World War. In the intervening years, a group of schools had emerged that might be broadly described as humanistic. These schools were roughly contemporary, sharing several common beliefs about the 'true' nature of humanity.

In attempting to summarize the contributions made by the principal figures in humanistic psychology, several major themes emerge. Firstly, most humanists preferred to work directly with the conscious mind during therapy; thus, they can be viewed as an offshoot of the ego analyst tradition begun by Alfred Adler and his disciples. Humanistic psychotherapists were less preoccupied with 'unconscious motivation' and exhibited a much greater willingness to accept the patient's 'word' as an adequate barometer of mental state. Secondly, all humanistic schools of psychotherapy stress that psychological problems are influenced by thinking. Mental illness, therefore, might be understood in terms of mental events, mental processes and mental structures. Finally and most importantly, the philosophical foundations of humanism posit that humanity is fundamentally good and rational.

Although the so-called 'third force' was a recognizable presence in psychology from the 1960s onward, its influence was remarkably limited, most notably in Europe. Why was this the case?

Firstly, humanism suffered from the same egocentricity that

afflicted psychoanalysis after Freud. Every few years a figurehead would introduce a new therapy, giving the appearance of diverging opinion. A result of this was that a group of approaches to treatment (sharing many common assumptions about the nature of the mind) were viewed as entirely separate. Unlike behaviourism, which has a sense of unity emerging from cumulative contributions to a main body of work, humanistic psychology appeared fragmented.

Secondly, mainstream psychologists and psychiatrists tended to view this new group of therapies as the work of fringe practitioners. This uncharitable view was certainly reinforced by the somewhat maverick nature of humanism's leading representatives, most notably Fritz Perls.

Finally, both psychoanalysis and behaviourism were part of strong traditions that could be traced back to the nineteenth century. Moreover, they were preparing to do battle. Humanistic psychology represented not only a late arrival, but also a late arrival that, as far as academic psychology and psychiatry were concerned, had arrived at a most inopportune moment. As two weighty traditions were about to collide, interest was firmly focused on the main event.

The most striking feature of third force writing is its faith in the redeeming qualities of humanity. 'Goodness' and 'rationality' provide the firm bedrock, upon which outstanding achievements can be built. The human race is positive, forward-looking, with virtually unlimited potential for growth. The evangelical zeal that characterizes humanistic writing is, on reflection, startling – Startling, because humanism gained momentum in a world that had just witnessed Auschwitz and Hiroshima. The fact that these moral catastrophes should have heralded the appearance of a movement, a fundamental tenet of which was 'man is good', seems almost inexplicable. Yet, it is very likely that Sigmund Freud would not have been reluctant to offer an explanation. The old cynic would have almost certainly suggested that humanists were collectively confirming the cornerstone of psychoanalysis: the existence of defences such as denial and reaction formation.

The military historian Quincey Wright has calculated that, since the twelfth century, war in Europe has steadily increased.

His calculations take into account the duration of war, the size of the forces involved, and the proportion of combatants relative to the total population and numbers of casualties. This horrific escalation over a period of nearly a thousand years reached its tormented climax in the Second World War. To suggest, in the afterglow of Auschwitz and Hiroshima, that humanity is fundamentally good, seems to be both hopelessly naive and hollow. By 1945, Freud's grim view of humanity had been more than vindicated. Whatever the general weaknesses of the psychoanalytic view, in this respect psychoanalysis seemed to be correct. Humanity shared far more with its animal ancestry than it cared to acknowledge. Freud's ideological heir, Melanie Klein, had described tiny infants, biting and raging at the 'bad breast'. On reflection, bringing the world to the brink of destruction seems far more the handiwork of Klein's ferocious infants than the self-actualizing new-age progeny of the third force.

On 25 July 1886, on the Lindengracht of Amsterdam's Jordaan district, a policeman tried to halt a traditional eel-pulling contest, a tug of war using a live eel smeared with soap to make it more slippery. The participants were angered by the policeman's objections and a crowd convened to manhandle the constable into a cellar where he was held captive. When news of this reached the officer in charge, reinforcements were sent in. When they arrived on the Lindengracht, they were showered with flower pots and roof tiles. The police retaliated and a skirmish became a battle. The crowd rioted and the army were eventually summoned to establish some kind of order. The 'battle' lasted for three days. Hundreds were injured and 26 people were killed.

Perhaps humanity is neither good nor rational. Perhaps, it is impossible to reconcile human history with humanistic optimism; however, in a godless universe, bereft of a moral framework and the comforting hallmarks of design, it was inevitable that humanity should invest itself with the godlike properties of goodness and rationality. Someone, after all, must attempt to find order in the chaos.

The humanists, with their intellectualization of suffering, are part of a philosophical tradition that extends back to Aristotle;

however, they may also be part of another Greek tradition. They have inadvertently re-enacted an ancient mythological drama. Like Prometheus, they have stolen divine fire and given it to humanity. The illusions of goodness and rationality still provide comfort and warmth, in a world that has witnessed far crueller fire.

CHAPTER 6

The Mind Regained

'Furthermore, whenever we hold the belief that something
is terrible or fearsome, we at once experience the corresponding emotion, as also with comforting beliefs.'

Aristotle, *De Anima*

Among the stately, time-hallowed reaches of Hatfield House in
Hertfordshire hangs Isaac Oliver's *Rainbow Portrait* of Queen
Elizabeth the First. It is a portrait ripe with symbolism. The
cold, haughty queen holds a rainbow in her hand, announcing
that she has brought peace to an England divided by
schismatics. On the sleeve of her rich gown, there is an emblem
that could be aptly appropriated to signal the state of
psychotherapy midway through the twentieth century.
Elizabeth's sleeve is embroidered with a snake, representing
wisdom. From its mouth dangles a ruby heart on a gold chain.
The queen's head clearly has sovereignty over her heart.

In the post-war years, the dangling heart of human emotion
had been secured in the snake's mouth by a generation of
humanists; however, their intellectualization of suffering had
exerted only a weak influence on the course and development
of psychotherapy. The third force was as much in need of a
rainbow portrait as Elizabethan England. Someone was needed
who would draw together the various threads of humanistic
thinking, and present them in a coherent, credible and
authoritative way. When that someone emerged – an unlikely,
congenial figure, with a shock of white hair and a penchant for
red bow ties – he become the most influential figure in the
world of psychotherapy since Sigmund Freud.

Aaron Temkin Beck was born in 1921, the son of two Russian

Jewish immigrants. He was raised in New England and showed
academic promise from an early age. After training in
medicine and psychiatry, Beck completed a psychoanalytic
training at the Philadelphia Psychoanalytic Institute from
which he graduated in 1958. He became an assistant professor
of psychiatry at Pennsylvania State University in 1959.

Beck's first research interest was the scientific investigation
of psychoanalytic theory. Bowlby had only recently completed
his early work on maternal deprivation and it seemed that the
systematic study of Freudian ideas might, at last, acquire a
certain amount of respectability, particularly in those circles
frequented by the mandarins of the scientific establishment.

Beck's preliminary studies were very much within the
tradition of experimental psychology, a tradition that emulated
mainstream science by employing the experiment as the
principal means of testing hypotheses. Beck would give patients
tasks and observe their reactions in a laboratory-type setting.
Such reactions might be consistent or inconsistent with a
particular idea drawn from psychoanalytic theory. Thus,
features of the theory could be either confirmed, or
alternatively, refuted. This is quite different from the method
of enquiry endorsed by Freud himself, which was to gather
information by simply observing patients during their
psychotherapy sessions.

Although Beck's initial findings were entirely consistent with
psychoanalytic theory, his research programme soon began to
yield discrepant results. Indeed, as his work progressed he
found himself presiding over a body of data showing that – at
least with respect to the features of psychoanalytic theory
under investigation – Freud was wrong. Understandably, Beck
became somewhat disillusioned with psychoanalysis. By the late
1950s, he had begun to develop his own framework within
which he could understand and treat psychological problems.
He had been particularly impressed by the writings of George
Kelly; however, it is alleged that Beck's ideas on the origins of
mental illness became sharply focused during the course of a
single therapeutic session that occurred in 1959.

Beck was listening to a depressed young man who was
free-associating in the manner recommended by Freud. Quite

suddenly, the young man became extremely angry. He began to shout at his therapist. Beck remained calm and asked him how he was feeling? The patient replied: *Guilty*. After further questioning, it transpired that while the young man had been shouting at Beck, he had simultaneously experienced a string of self-critical thoughts such as 'I shouldn't have said that', 'I'm wrong to criticize him', 'I'm bad' and 'He won't like me'.

These self-critical thoughts had occurred at the very same time the young man was expressing anger. It was as though they were automatic, like a tape recorder being played inside his head. Moreover, the patient's anger did not lead directly to feelings of guilt. Instead, guilt was experienced as a consequence of this second, automatic train of thought. Beck, like his immediate predecessor Albert Ellis, was struck by the close relationship between thinking and feeling.

Beck investigated the phenomenon of automatic thinking in other patients. He found that they too were experiencing thoughts during sessions which they usually failed to disclose. It was as though each patient, while free-associating, was also listening to a running commentary or internal monologue. Moreover, it was this internal monologue that seemed to be the most important determinant of mood.

Between 1960 and 1964 Beck began to develop a framework for understanding his patients' experiences. This was an explicitly 'cognitive' framework, in which *negative automatic thoughts* were given special significance. Beck abandoned insight as the principal therapeutic objective. Moreover, he replaced interpretation with the direct modification of thoughts. As such, the practice of Beck's therapy was very similar to rational emotive therapy. Unhelpful thoughts were recognized and then disputed or challenged.

Beck's ideas aroused little interest. He gave talks to psychoanalysts, most of whom simply walked out. He also gave talks to psychiatrists, who responded with an indifference close to contempt. In the early 1960s, psychiatry was enjoying a revival of interest in biological, or drug-based treatments for psychological problems; subsequently, Beck's ideas seemed anachronistic. Even so, he continued to develop his new therapy. Indeed, demonstrating a remarkably sanguine disposition, Beck established a small research group in order to test the effectiveness of his treatment techniques. Thus, by the time behaviour therapists were walking out of his lectures, Beck had become quite accustomed to being treated as a maverick; however, both psychotherapy and the world it occupied were changing. Although Beck was largely unaware of these changes, the cultural climate was becoming more and more favourable for his ascendence.

After a very promising start, behaviour therapy had unexpectedly encountered both theoretical and practical difficulties. By the late 1960s and early 1970s, doubts had been raised concerning the role of conditioning experiences in the acquisition of irrational fears, and more importantly, it was becoming increasingly obvious that certain psychological problems could not be treated using only behavioural techniques. Something else was necessary. These problems were not important enough to halt the progress of behaviour therapy; however, they were of sufficient importance to make many practitioners stop and re-evaluate their approach.

Since the time of John Watson, behaviourists had accepted that phobias were nothing more than classically conditioned emotional responses. Therefore, it should be possible to trace the development of any phobia back to a specific learning event, in which fear and an innocuous stimulus become associated. As behaviour therapists gained more experience in the clinic, it became apparent that although many phobic patients could remember conditioning incidents, a vast number could not. How could this inconsistency be explained? How was it possible for conditioned responses to be established in the absence of conditioning experiences?

Initially, it was suggested that the discrepancy between Watson's theory and patient testimony was illusory. Watson was indeed correct; however, many patients were simply unable to remember the critical conditioning event. This was a deeply unsatisfactory explanation and only the most evangelical behaviourists were convinced by it. What then were the alternatives? One possibility was that those patients who were unable to recall conditioning experiences had been born with irrational fears. This was, of course, unspeakable heresy to 'learning' theorists. A further possibility (and one much less offensive to behavioural sensibilities) was that some patients had acquired their irrational fears by watching others (for example, a parent). This latter view was promulgated by the psychologist Albert Bandura, whose principal academic interest was *social learning*, that is, the kind of learning that occurs when one human being watches another. Bandura was very much within the behavioural camp; however, his work represented a shift away from the Pavlovian and Skinnerian traditions. He had begun to explain behaviour by emphasizing the role of cognition.

Bandura developed a treatment procedure called *modelling*, based on the apparent facility with which human beings assimilate socially transmitted information. It was originally used to help individuals who were fearful of snakes. Such individuals would observe (or watch a film) of others approaching a snake. The people featured in these confrontations, known as models, gradually moved closer to the snake and were clearly able to cope with the situation. After viewing these events and films, phobic patients experienced a significant reduction in fear. These improvements were difficult to explain from a pure behavioural perspective. Desirable behaviours were not being reinforced, no procedure was being employed to inhibit anxiety, nor were there any attempts at direct exposure to the feared situation. It seemed that modelling simply caused fearful subjects to change their minds.

In addition to these developments, the limitations of behaviour therapy were becoming more obvious. Although behaviour therapy proved to be an excellent treatment for anxiety disorders, it seemed to be much less effective when used to treat depression. Indeed, when depressed patients were put on Skinnerian 'reinforcement' schedules – in which the occurrence of a smile or participation in a group activity was rewarded – only modest improvements in overall mood were observed. These and other disappointing results prompted many behaviour therapists to renege on the first principle of behaviourism. They began to refer to the mental state of their patients. More precisely, they were taking an interest in what their patients were thinking.

This interest in mental events eventually resulted in the curious phenomenon of behavioural psychologists developing treatment techniques that relied on the modification of thought. Psychologists such as Donald Meichenbaum and his colleagues were using *self-instructional training* (SIT) to address a range of problems, most notably difficulty coping with stress. This approach involved the rehearsal of helpful internal instructions, such as 'Slow down' or 'Take a deep breath and relax'.

Self-instruction proved particularly helpful with respect to the treatment of impulsive or hyperactive children. Hyperactivity is a problem that arises in early childhood and is particularly associated with concentration difficulties. First, the child was taught to imitate a desired behaviour. Then the behaviour was repeated while the child spoke out aloud a set of given instructions. These usually described the sequence of steps required to complete the task in hand. The child was then asked to perform the behaviour while whispering these self-instructions, and finally the desired behaviour while just 'thinking' the instructions. This type of therapy began to be described as *cognitive behavioural therapy* or *behaviour modification*.

Unfortunately, not everyone within the behavioural establishment was happy with these new developments. Wolpe and Skinner were perhaps the most outspoken, lambasting those who dared reintroduce the sullied concept of 'mentalism' back into scientific psychology. By the mid-1970s, the role of thinking in behaviour therapy was a source of considerable debate, one that was to precipitate a good deal of political activity reminiscent of the intrigues that dogged the early years of the psychoanalytic movement.

Readings in 'cognitive behaviour modification' were prohibited in some graduate psychology programmes. Moreover, the board of the Association for Advancement of Behaviour Therapy mooted whether those with cognitive interests should be allowed to address conferences. Some demanded that dissidents be expelled from the organization. Contributions with a cognitive bias were banned from several publications and *The Journal of Applied Behavioural Analysis* would not accept articles that so much as used the word cognitive. Attempting to ban this word now seems particularly ridiculous, because psychology was, in fact, in the throes of a transformation what would later be described as the cognitive revolution.

The reason for this intellectual *coup d'état* was the advent and subsequent ubiquity of the computer. While Viktor Frankl had been observing his fellow prisoners in Auschwitz and contemplating 'meaning', the war effort had required the development of machines that could also discern 'meaning' of a very different kind; the 'meaning' of the coded messages that kept Berlin in touch with the furthest outposts of the Third Reich. In the unlikely location of Bletchley, England, the first electronic valve computer was set to work. Colossus could accomplish tasks within minutes that would have previously occupied a team of cryptographers for weeks. The war effort gave information-processing technology a huge boost, and in the 1950s the wider application of computers was soon recognized; however, what was not immediately recognized was that the computer also provided a particularly powerful metaphor for the working mind.

In the nineteenth century, the mechanisms that govern thinking had been explained by comparing them with clockwork, hydraulics and the telephone exchange. These weak analogues were very much superseded by the computer. Indeed, the very language of information-processing technology revived interest in cognitive psychology. Academics began to talk of 'storage capacity' instead of memory and 'retrieval' instead of remembering. Armed with a new vocabulary, greater opportunities arose for detailed descriptions of mental processes.

The recognition among some behaviour therapists of the inadequacies of pure behaviourism, combined with the cognitive revolution in psychology, provided an ideal climate for the emergence of a method of changing minds that was sympathetic with these developments. Beck had decided to call his new treatment *cognitive therapy*. He could not have chosen a name that possessed a more satisfying contemporary resonance.

In the mid-1970s, Beck was invited to address the 'Society for Psychotherapy Research'. He was to talk in a routine symposium and expected the usual rather disinterested response from the audience. Beck had brought only 25 information handouts to the meeting; a number which he considered adequate. On this particular occasion, he was rather surprised that the lecture hall had begun to fill. Indeed, there were several hundred in attendance. He was prompted to ask a colleague what so many people were doing there. 'Dr Beck,' replied his colleague, 'they've come to see you.' Beck's initial response was disbelief; however, the tide of opinion had suddenly changed. The popularity of cognitive therapy has been increasing ever since.

In 1976, Beck summarized his work in a book entitled *Cognitive Therapy and the Emotional Disorders*. In retrospect, it must be ranked with classics such as Breuer and Freud's *Studies on Hysteria* or Wolpe's *Psychotherapy by Reciprocal Inhibition*; however, in spite of its great influence, Beck's book contains very few genuinely new or original ideas. It is perhaps best considered a very lucid synthesis of trends that had been developing in American existential and humanistic psychotherapy since the 1940s and 1950s. Nevertheless, Beck seemed to express these ideas with greater authority than his predecessors. He submitted persuasive research findings showing that cognitive therapy could be as effective a treatment for depression as medication. Moreover, his style was direct and modern. He clearly held the view that the mind processed information in much the same way as a computer and that 'faulty processing' could account for what psychologists and psychiatrists called mental illness.

The philosophical tenor of Beck's work is optimistic. He has stated that people have free will and can change, that people have a responsibility to change and that they will change. This determined assault on pessimism makes him a modern standard-bearer of the humanistic tradition. In the opening pages of *Cognitive Therapy and the Emotional Disorders*, Beck proclaims: 'Man has the key to understanding and solving his psychological disturbance within the scope of his own awareness.' These words could be embedded anywhere in an essay by Carl Rogers without trammelling its inspirational velocity.

According to Beck, emotional disorders are characterized by streams of involuntary negative automatic thoughts (NATs). In problems such as anxiety these thoughts are about threat and danger, whereas in depression these thoughts may reflect themes to do with loss, failure or worthlessness. In Beck's scheme, NATs have certain distinctive characteristics. They occur rapidly and with little or no effort. Indeed, Beck originally referred to them as an example of 'thoughtless thought'. Patients often describe them as 'coming out of the blue' or just 'popping into the mind'.

When NATs occur, they seem very plausible. Thus, an individual suffering from social anxiety might become aware of the thought: 'I really look stupid and people are watching me.' He or she is unlikely to question this at the time. NATs can, after many repetitions, occur in shorthand. Therefore, the above example might enter awareness in an abbreviated form: 'look stupid . . . people watching.' Another way of construing NATs is to regard them as a kind of mental habit.

Like Ellis, Beck observed a particularly close relationship between thought and emotion; however, he also suggested that particular types of psychological problem are associated with particular thoughts or ideas. Therefore, an individual who experiences NATs about 'falling from a high place' will very likely suffer from acrophobia (i.e. fear of heights), whereas a person who experiences NATs about 'suffocating' will very likely suffer from claustrophobia (i.e. fear of enclosed spaces). The technical term used to describe the thematic link between thoughts and symptoms is content specificity.

An anxious patient might experience NATs about dying in a plane crash, but also experience NATs about dying from a brain tumour. Although these NATs concern different threats, they are very similar insofar as they both show an exaggerated belief in the likelihood of certain dangers. In much the same way as a fairground mirror might reliably compress or elongate a reflected image, so it is that the perturbed mind systematically distorts thinking. Beck called these distortions *systematic logical errors*. Terms such as overgeneralization and misattribution –

both introduced many years earlier by Rogers and Ellis – describe logical errors; however, Beck's contribution was to compile a much more exhaustive list. For example, *personalization* describes the logical error that results in persistent self-blame. Thus, an individual will see a causal relationship between his or her own actions and subsequent negative events even when there is no actual connection. *Dichotomous thinking* (also termed black-and-white thinking) occurs when an individual cannot see the middle ground. Events tend to be interpreted as either wonderful or awful. Beck described many more thinking errors of this kind.

Cognitive psychologists were interested in Beck's list of thinking errors, because they seemed to be consistent with an information-processing (or computer-inspired) account of the mind. The factors that influenced the errors of judgement common in those suffering from mental illness could be understood in terms of features and processes routinely discussed by computer scientists. For example, depressed individuals might actually 'store' more negative information in 'memory' than non-depressed individuals. Moreover, such information might be more easily 'retrieved'. Thus, evaluating the meaning of events and interpreting experience will be influenced by characteristics of the 'database' and the kind of system 'operating' on it. Beck's clinical observations and the contemporary fashion for using the computer as a metaphor for the mind married very well.

Beck's account of psychological problems was not limited to the occurrence of negative automatic thoughts and their systematic distortions. He also posited a second, deeper level of cognition. This deeper level consists of rigid and unhelpful beliefs. When such beliefs are linked together with respect to a certain theme, Beck refers to them as *schemas*. Thus, Bartlett's term is used to imply the presence of 'mental structures', which can influence both cognitive events (e.g. NATs) and cognitive processes (e.g. attention and recollection).

It has already been suggested that schemas can exist for concepts highly relevant to mental illness, for example, 'failure' or 'worthlessness'. An individual with a 'failure' schema will 'process' information associated with the idea of failure very efficiently. For example, he or she might be quick to notice any facial expressions in others that suggest disappointment. He or she will find it relatively easy to remember past experiences of failure. Moreover, he or she will probably experience many NATs on the theme of failure (such as 'I can't do it' or 'I'm useless'). By incorporating schemas into his framework, Beck was tacitly paying homage to Kelly, whose construct system has a virtually identical function in personal construct theory.

Beck suggested that the fundamental beliefs characteristic of individuals suffering from emotional problems are rigid and inflexible. Such rigidity of belief tends to be less common in healthy individuals. Beck found that during the course of therapy, unhelpful beliefs become more obvious. They – as it were – rise to the surface. He also noticed that such beliefs often took the form of 'if-then' statements. That is, they are *propositions* that refer to a particular outcome if a particular *condition* is met. An example is: 'If I express my opinion then others will be offended.' Beck described this kind of belief as a *dysfunctional assumption*; however, contemporary cognitive therapists also refer to a level of cognition that exists at a still deeper level. This is the level of the *core belief*. These take the form of stark, *non-conditional* statements, such as 'I am unlovable'. Core beliefs probably become consolidated in very early childhood. They tend to have a more pervasive affect than dysfunctional assumptions, influencing not only mood (e.g. depression) but also many aspects of an individual's personality (e.g. ability to maintain intimate relationships).

Schemas are formed as a result of learning experiences; however, once established as part of the cognitive architecture, they do not necessarily exert an immediate influence on an individual's thinking and subsequent behaviour. Indeed, schemas can remain dormant for many years. They are usually activated by an event that is, in some way, similar to the original learning experience (i.e. the event or events responsible for belief formation).

A typical example of this phenomenon might concern a woman who, as a child, listened to repeated unfavourable comparisons made between herself and her sibling. This might result in the formation of a core belief, such as 'I am inferior', and several attendant dysfunctional assumptions, one of which might be 'If I am not valued by others then I am worthless'. Even though an 'inferiority' schema may have been created, it may not yet influence the occurrence of negative automatic thoughts and cause a depressive illness; however, the dormant schema may be activated by a critical event, for example, marital breakdown. Once the inferiority schema is 'active' it will facilitate the entry into awareness of NATs. Examples are 'I'm going to be alone for ever', 'It's all my fault' and 'I can't handle life'. Needless to say, the presence of this class of mental event will almost inevitably lower mood.

Beck reiterated an observation previously made by many other therapists regarding the relationship between language and emotion. Certain judgemental or 'extreme' words, either appearing in the stream of consciousness or embedded within a 'dysfunctional assumption' or core belief, are likely to be associated with disturbed mood. Horney's 'tyranny of shoulds' and Ellis' 'must-urbating' have already been encountered; however, Beck noted many other similar examples such as 'ought', 'always', and 'never'. Such words place an excessive demand on the individual and also amplify thinking errors. The depressed individual who experiences the thought of 'I never get anything right' is clearly misrepresenting the truth. The likelihood of having progressed beyond infancy without *ever* having performed a correct response or behaviour in *all* situations is of course vanishingly small.

It has already been suggested that the technique employed by Beck in therapy sessions resembled the 'disputing' originally developed by Ellis; however, in cognitive therapy, disputing (or challenging) is practised within a framework informed by two major principles. The first of these Beck described as *collaborative empiricism.*

Beck urged burgeoning cognitive therapists to abandon the inequalities of the traditional doctor–patient relationship and to cultivate instead a 'collaborative' dialogue. Therapist and patient work together, attempting to establish which thoughts are accurate and which are distorted. This process should be empirical, with both parties agreeing on 'experiments' that will prove or disprove particular thoughts or beliefs.

Thus, a lift phobic might make a prediction that he or she will suffocate in a lift. The cognitive therapist does not automatically say, 'No you won't', but rather, 'How can we test this?' An initial suggestion might be to observe the effects of sitting in a lift-like enclosed space on respiration. Such an experiment might involve the patient sitting for ten minutes in a small room without windows. After a number of similar experiments, the patient's beliefs about the likelihood of suffocation may be less rigid, and he or she may be willing to undertake the definitive experiment: getting into a lift. The concept of 'collaborative empiricism' shares much common ground with Kelly's view of 'man as scientist' and marks a large area of overlap between cognitive therapy and personal construct psychology.

The second fundamental principle that guides the practice of cognitive therapy is *Socratic questioning*. In Plato's many works depicting Socrates, the great philosopher is shown to have practised a particular method of getting to the truth. When presented with an adversary, Socrates rarely argued a point, but merely asked his opponent a series of carefully chosen questions. These usually revealed either inconsistencies or weaknesses. The end point of such a debate usually involved the adversary having to conclude himself that he had been mistaken. In other words, Socrates rarely started off by saying, 'I am right and you are wrong', but rather, 'Let us examine the strengths and weaknesses of your position'. He would then help his adversary to test his favoured beliefs. Beck saw many similarities between debate, as it took place in the Athenian market place, and clinical practice in Philadelphia! Moreover, Socrates' method of helping his adversaries to understand their own thinking errors provided an ideal model for good clinical practice.

The practice of cognitive therapy has far more in common with the pragmatic, directive approach of behaviour therapy than with the insight-based approach of psychoanalysis. During the first sessions of cognitive therapy, the patient is introduced to unfamiliar terms, such as 'negative automatic thoughts', and basic principles are discussed. The patient is given diaries on which to record the co-occurence of negative thoughts and emotional discomfort. In subsequent sessions, the close relationship between thoughts and feelings is discussed and thinking errors are pointed out. The validity of negative thoughts and beliefs are tested using the Socratic method and behavioural experiments. Over time, the patient begins to replace negative automatic thoughts with more accurate thoughts. Therapy may then shift to a deeper level and attempts might then be made to uncover dysfunctional assumptions and unhelpful core beliefs. Once the patient is aware of these, they too can be modified using Socratic questioning and experiment.

Prior to the expansion of cognitive therapy, the term cognitive behavioural therapy described an approach to treatment endorsed by behaviour therapists who were also willing to work with 'rehearsed' thoughts or 'self-instruction'. Today, cognitive behavioural therapy has a slightly different meaning. Although the behavioural element remains relatively unchanged, the cognitive element is now almost always 'Beckian' in flavour. Thus, cognitive behavioural therapists tend to practise both cognitive and behavioural therapy. The conflation of these two approaches can be attributed to the fact that, at least at the practice level, cognitive and behaviour therapy share much common ground. Both are directive therapies that have strong links with academic psychology. The conflation of the behavioural and cognitive communities has also resulted in a very large number of therapists describing themselves as cognitive behavioural in orientation.

Beck, like Freud, managed to link and integrate a number of pre-existing ideas into a coherent whole, and more importantly, he had the good fortune to be undertaking this task at exactly the right time. Although some of Beck's followers have suggested that he developed most of his ideas in isolation, this seems somewhat implausible. Moreover, the breadth of vision required to see how numerous disparate ideas can be brought together within a single framework is sufficiently impressive to require no apologists.

The comparison made between Beck and Freud is one that warrants more than superficial consideration. Both men came from Jewish backgrounds. Both men were originally dismissed by the medical establishment. Both suffered – albeit intermittently – from neurotic illnesses. In Beck's case, they were fear of injury, heights, suffocation and public speaking. Finally, Beck, like Freud, has his own 'Antigone', that is to say, a devoted daughter who continues to develop and promote her father's work.

In spite of these many similarities between Beck and Freud, they differ decisively in one respect. Unlike Freud, Beck has not suffered from ambitious schismatics. Indeed, on the whole, those with an interest in cognitive therapy have only ever attempted to develop the approach by building on previous work. As such, cognitive therapy continues to grow. There are now cognitive theories, based on Beck's original approach, that explain the development of symptoms in a wide range of psychological disorders. Moreover, each of these theories has inspired slight modifications of treatment technique, most of which have proved very effective. In the hands of a dedicated army of disciples, Beck's techniques have been refined, elaborated and tested the world over. Recently, cognitive therapists have strayed from the traditional territory of anxiety and depression on to new ground, namely, the modification of delusions in psychiatric problems such as schizophrenia. Preliminary investigations suggests that even those suffering from severe mental illnesses can be helped, at least in part, by cognitive therapy.

The fact that cognitive therapy has expanded without significant fragmentation is largely attributable to Beck himself. He is noted for his personal charm and humility. He once, for example, went to see Albert Ellis for a session of rational emotive therapy to help him with his public speaking. There can be few figureheads of note who would openly consult an individual who might be described as a competitor. Moreover, in the company of other figureheads, Beck is uniquely open-minded. He has never been a fundamentalist, so therapists have felt comfortable modifying and developing treatment techniques within a cognitive framework. Compare this with Freud, who while feigning a permissive attitude, disapproved of any disciple who dared to question his views on the sexual origin of mental illness. Finally, unlike many of his humanist predecessors, Beck is eminently respectable. There is nothing of the fringe in Beck's writings.

There can be little doubt that cognitive therapy and its almost indistinguishable relative cognitive behavioural therapy have become the dominant (and arguably the most successful) forms of psychotherapy to be practised in the twentieth century; however, in spite of these advances, the lay population is remarkably ill-informed. Media representations of psychotherapy remain predominantly psychoanalytic. From the humble newspaper cartoon to the Hollywood movie, patients still recline on countless couches and disclose their innermost secrets.

Fifty years or so after Freud's early work was published, a randomly selected member of the general public would almost certainly be familiar with the name of Sigmund Freud; he or she might also know something of psychoanalysis (even if such knowledge were expressed in terms of the props, such as the couch, rather than the procedure). Psychotherapy has been evolving and splintering throughout the course of the twentieth century. Now, some fifty years or so after some radical changes in the theory and practice of psychotherapy, a randomly selected member of the general public would look very perplexed if asked to identify Aaron Beck. He or she would also know little, if anything, about cognitive therapy.

In Martin Amis' novel, *The Information*, he suggests that every century, with increasing awareness of the true size of the cosmos, the human race gets smaller. This statement has also proved true for psychotherapists. Like Jonathan Swift's eponymous hero in *Gulliver's Travels*, they have journeyed from Lilliput to Brobdingnag. Freud believed that psychoanalysis had laid bare the principal forces that shaped human culture and civilization. This is reflected in his writings, which contain essays on diverse subjects such as art, literature, religion and war. Adler believed that his ideas might precipitate major social changes, while Jung, in visionary mode, claimed to have glimpsed eternity through the portal of his own consciousness. The late post-Freudians were diminished in stature, although some, like Klein, still retained a modicum of cultural celebrity. Indeed, a West End play featuring Melanie Klein was still able to draw large audiences in the 1980s; however, Klein was probably the last therapist of real significance to earn public recognition (there have, of course, been numerous controversial figures who have claimed their moment of fame, but whose impact on the development of psychotherapy has been negligible). After the 1950s, the representatives of humanism and behaviourism become faceless individuals. Today, the most influential psychotherapist in the world is largely unknown outside the parochial domain of clinical psychology and psychiatry.

Post-war developments in psychotherapy have been instrumental with respect to shaping current understanding of the mind, emotion and the nature of human suffering; however, these important developments have aroused negligible public interest. The man with the beard, with the Viennese accent and with the penetrating eyes still towers over his progeny. Why is it that Freud's ideas have saturated western culture so thoroughly?

Psychoanalysis is the primogenitor of all contemporary psychotherapy. Thus, Freud retains the special status afforded to all originals (even though several similar ideas were being discussed by now largely forgotten individuals such as Moritz Benedickt and Pierre Janet many years earlier). Moreover, psychoanalysis is highly memorable. Ideas such as the Oedipus complex have settled comfortably on an existing cultural underlay that has been systematically enriched since the time of Sophocles; however, even the trappings of psychoanalysis – such as the fabled couch and the reclining patient – leave a curiously durable impression in the mind. The peculiar arrangement of a fully clothed, supine individual, revealing intimate secrets to a detached observer, possesses, perhaps, some of the haunting qualities that make the work of dramatists such as Harold Pinter so memorable.

In addition, psychoanalysis combines mystery and narrative, two qualities that have the power to excite curiosity. In the unconscious, nothing is what it seems to be; however, with the analyst's help, forbidden knowledge is revealed in the traffic of dreams. The night is forced to concede its secrets. Moreover, every symptom – from a nervous cough to suicidal depression – conceals a story. It is a story that progresses, almost inexorably, to a satisfying conclusion in which everything is explained. When Freud 'wraps up' a case, we are never far from territory also occupied by Sherlock Holmes and Hercule Poirot. Compare this with the theory and practice of contemporary psychotherapy. There is no contest. Psychoanalysis is simply more interesting. So much so that the majority are prepared to forgive it for being mostly wrong!

Finally, the history of psychoanalysis itself has become a romance. Consider, for example, the images evoked by the early years of discovery: enigmatic Anna O. drifting into altered states of consciousness and whispering 'tormenting, tormenting', while Freud and Breuer teeter on the edge of an abyss that is nothing less than the darkest depths of the human mind. Earnest young men who, while seeking merely to heal the sick, inadvertently stumble upon arcane knowledge of universal significance. Psychoanalysis can boast a body of correspondence that reads like an epistolary novel: alliances, rivalry and bitter betrayal. The intellectual landscape of psychoanalysis, and the people who witnessed its nativity, are bathed in the dying light of nineteenth-century romanticism.

The contemporary model of the mind (and the method of psychotherapy that it has produced) lacks drama. The brain is a soft computer and suffering can be reduced to conditioning or biased information processing. For most, this is profoundly unflattering. Perhaps it is for this reason, more than any other, that psychotherapy over the last fifty years has never attracted the audience originally won by Freud.

Psychoanalysis placed the source of suffering in the id. Anxiety and depression could ultimately be attributed to the most fundamental, animal passions, elemental forces of sexuality and aggression. Behaviourism reduced suffering to a reflex, a learned response. The individual is the hapless victim of circumstance and chance, a puppet manipulated by the tug and release of environmental strings. Finally, humanistic approaches attribute suffering to the intellect. The degree to which an experience is painful will be determined by how that experience is appraised. In psychoanalysis, suffering is caused by an uncontrollable force on the inside. According to behavioural principles, suffering is caused by an uncontrollable force on the outside; however, within the context of humanistic, cognitive psychotherapy, suffering is a choice, a decision. Since the middle of the twentieth century, humanity has been far more willing to take responsibility for suffering. This suggests, that in some ways at least, humanity is growing up.

Psychotherapy may no longer be as glamorous as it once was, but it is now a more mature discipline. It has abandoned grandiose claims. Figures like Aaron Beck have little interest in delivering the third blow to humanity, destroying religion, or commenting on the works of Goethe and Leonardo da Vinci. Beck's aspirations have always been far more modest: to understand how the mind works, and to develop an efficient method of ameliorating suffering. Beck will never challenge Freud as a cultural icon, nor will he ever capture the imagination of the general public; nevertheless, it is very likely that his method of treating psychological problems will continue to be practised for many decades to come, and perhaps, be even more enduring than the original talking cure.

CHAPTER 7

Divided by a Common Language

'Seek Love in the Pity of others' Woe, In the gentle relief of another's care.'

William Blake, *The Pickering Manuscript*

Studies on Hysteria by Breuer and Freud was the first major work ever written on the subject of psychotherapy. When their labours were completed, its two authors – not only colleagues but also by that time close friends – turned their attention to the preface. In the first edition it contains only four paragraphs, the last of which is something of an apology: 'If at some points divergent and indeed contradictory opinions are expressed, this is not to be regarded as evidence of any fluctuations in our views. It arises from the natural and justifiable differences between the opinions of two observers who are agreed upon the facts and their basic reading of them, but who are not invariably at one in their interpretations and conjectures.'

The 'natural and justifiable differences' of opinion referred to by Breuer and Freud eventually destroyed their friendship. Within a few years, such differences had all but destroyed the Vienna Psychoanalytic Society. Thereafter, psychotherapists have never been able to unite under a single banner. Schisms, witch-hunts, expulsions and purges have all posed a significant threat to the reputation and credibility of an already beleaguered profession.

One of the most contentious arguments in the medieval world concerned the conflict between intuitive and intellectual approaches to worship. This conflict was eventually dramatized when Bernard of Clairvaux (later to become St Bernard) and Peter Abelard (a great scholar) took part in the medieval equivalent of a world heavyweight title fight. For Bernard, the spiritual path was unequivocally intuitive; however, for Abelard, it could only ever be cerebral. Today, two medieval theologians engaged in such a debate would appear to share far more in common than their heated exchanges might suggest: belief in God, the redemptive properties of praying to the Virgin Mary, and hellfire, to name but a few. Whether or not the presence of God should be 'felt' or 'understood' seems an irrelevant detail, particularly when set against the commonalities of unshakable faith.

After a century of dissent, it is becoming increasingly apparent that the differences between various schools of psychotherapy are less consequential than originally thought. Indeed, many historic clashes have come to resemble the sterile arguments of medieval theologians. The distinctions made between Anna Freud and Melanie Klein, for example, shrink to near insignificance when their conjoint advocacy of child psychotherapy is considered. Similarly, the quarrels between pure behaviourists and the pioneers of behaviour modification now seem ludicrously overblown. Both approaches were, after all, distinctly 'behavioural'. It would seem that psychotherapists are much like the British and American peoples, supposedly described by George Bernard Shaw as 'divided by a common language'.

In his classic text of 1961, *Persuasion and Healing*, the psychiatrist Jerome Frank offers a penetrating analysis of the critical features of psychotherapy. He arrives at a disconcerting conclusion: the *specific* elements of any given psychotherapy are not the major precipitant of change. For example, it is not the resolution of Oedipal conflicts during psychoanalysis, nor the modification of negative thinking patterns during cognitive therapy, that lead to a reduction in anxiety symptoms. Rather, it is a set of *non-specific* factors, common to both forms of therapy. If this position were to be translated into a medical equivalent, Frank might be arguing that it is not intravenous drugs that heal, but rather the common method of administration, namely, puncturing the skin with a hypodermic needle.

What then are the common elements shared by all forms of psychotherapy? Frank describes four. Firstly, *an emotionally charged and confiding relationship*. Secondly, *a healing setting*. Thirdly, *a rationale that provides a plausible explanation for the patient's symptoms and suggests a method for resolving them*. Finally, a *'ritual' or procedure that requires the active participation of both patient and therapist, and that is believed to be the means of restoring the patient's health*.

Humanists, such as Carl Rogers, attributed almost magical restorative powers to relationships characterized by warmth and genuineness. Even Freud, who famously urged his acolytes to adopt the detached attitude of a surgeon, advised that such inscrutability should only be affected after '*regular rapport*' had been established with the patient. Contrary to expectations, research has shown that 'good' therapists, who practise different forms of psychotherapy, are more alike, than 'good' and 'bad' therapists trained within the same tradition. Moreover, patients who have been successfully treated rate the quality of the relationship with their therapist as the most important aspect of treatment.

Bowlby's work on attachment theory suggests that something akin to a re-parenting process might be taking place in all forms of psychotherapy; however, the therapeutic relationship may draw its potency from resonances that are far deeper and fundamental than mere personal history.

The geneticist Steve Jones reminds us that apes, whom we look to in order to see an earlier version of ourselves, spend an inordinate amount of time grooming. This very basic social activity communicates acceptance and evokes a sense of belonging. Early human beings may well have 'reassured their companions' by grooming; however, when hunting became the predominant method of acquiring food, the organization of hunting bands required larger and larger social groups. If grooming had been retained as the principal means of preserving group integrity, then over half of the group's time would be consumed in this single activity. The evolutionary solution was to select for a more efficient means of establishing emotional bonds and ties. Jones concludes: 'Speech, even primitive speech, is a much better way of calming one's fellows than is touch. The very first words – long before the ancestors of today's language – may have been words of comfort.'

If Jones is correct, then any intimate communication will evoke ancient memories, the ministry of careful fingers. Many millions of years after the first words were used in comfort, Eric Berne referred to simple verbal exchanges as *strokes*. When a psychotherapist 'strokes' a patient, he or she is being included in the group. The loneliness of the primordial night recedes. The patient belongs.

It is interesting that intimacy has become a much less accepted feature of everyday life (most obviously so in the industrialized western world); however, the decline of intimacy is a relatively recent phenomenon. For example, in the seventeenth century, 'bundling' was a common practice, particularly among the young betrothed of England, America and Holland. Couples would get into bed, fully clothed, to cuddle, talk and sleep together. This was considered no more risqué than a private conversation in the parlour; however, bundling was not merely restricted to courting couples. In *An Intimate History of Humanity*, Theodore Zeldin observes that, after church on Sunday, a husband might 'invite a visitor to bundle with his wife or daughters'. Remarkably, bundling remained an institution is some areas (most notably Cape Cod in Massachusetts) until 1827. The telephone, satellite broadcasting, e-mail and the Internet have made Marshall McLuhan's 'global village' a reality; but it is a village whose residents rarely 'touch'. Perhaps, in a world where intimacy is increasingly 'virtual', psychotherapy is meeting the requirements of an expanding market – the market for 'real' human contact.

Although Frank stresses that all forms of psychotherapy involve the formation of a confiding (or intimate) relationship, he also points out that such relationships are often *emotionally charged*. The arousal and discharge of emotion may be an extremely important element of the healing process.

Yet again, it was Freud and Breuer who first discussed the desirability of releasing pent-up or repressed emotion. Indeed, in their early work they frequently refer to catharsis. Unwanted emotions are 'purged' once they have been re-experienced.

The arousal of emotions during therapy might also make important memories more accessible. It is as though powerful feelings open pathways of recollection that are ordinarily blocked. Finally, emotional states seem to make the mind less rigid. In the same way that metal is more pliable when heated, unhelpful beliefs become more tractable when the temperature in therapy sessions is raised. Thus, unhelpful beliefs can be modified more easily.

Even pure behaviour therapy, an approach that refuses to enter into analytical discussion about feelings, employs as its principal weapon against anxiety disorders 'exposure therapy', a procedure that will almost certainly evoke a heightened state of emotion in the patient. It may be that during the course of an exposure session, the beliefs that underpin an irrational fear surface and spontaneously change because of certain 'corrective' features of the situation. For example, it is difficult to maintain the belief that an ant is a dangerous creature when it has been marching up and down a therapist's hand for an hour without causing harm. Perhaps, in an emotionally aroused state, the mind is more ready to change, and also more able to accommodate information that contradicts unhelpful beliefs. Clearly, the therapeutic effects of arousing strong feelings in therapy sessions can only be fully exploited if the patient and therapist enjoy a relationship in which there are no restrictions on the expression of emotion.

Frank's second common factor concerns the staging of treatment. He stresses that all forms of psychotherapy take place in a 'healing setting'. The purpose of these settings is to emphasize the therapist's prestige, and at the same time to strengthen the patient's positive expectations. The degree to which a patient has faith in the practitioner and his or her methods can be a major influence on the success of treatment.

Historically, the healing setting has been as much a part of the healing procedure (in the broadest possible sense) as the treatment method itself. For example, in the 'sleep temples' of ancient Egypt and Greece, patients slumbered while robed priests played music and sang or chanted healing words. This is not too dissimilar to the practice of psychiatry in the 1950s. In imposing Victorian buildings, white-coated doctors would use insulin to induce an artificial coma in patients suffering from schizophrenia, and while the patients slept, the doctors would perform arcane and mystifying rituals. Insulin coma is, of course, no more a treatment for schizophrenia than sleeping in a temple; nevertheless, both procedures were associated with some success. That the mind (and the body for that matter) can be 'fooled' into feeling 'better' may seem somewhat implausible; however, until relatively recently, virtually all of medicine depended on the manipulation of expectations to cure illness.

For thousands of years, physicians have endorsed and prescribed what are now known to be useless and often dangerous treatments: 'puking', strong purgatives, blood-letting, the eye of a newt, and ground-up leather from the sole of an old shoe (to name but an unsavoury few). Although such treatments were theoretically impotent, doctors retained their social status. There is only one explanation for this: the treatments worked! With respect to the vast majority of minor ailments, 'faith' in a physician's expertise is generally sufficient to promote healing. Remarkably, recent research suggests that the situation remains largely unchanged. Up to 20 per cent of general practioners prescribe drugs that they believe will have no effect on the condition being treated. The prescription is purely symbolic, given to encourage expectations of improvement.

The immense power of expectations to affect health is now routinely taken into account in all drug trials. Usually, when a new drug is tested for effectiveness, its performance is compared with a placebo. This is a pill that looks identical to the real drug under investigation, but is made from a completely inert substance, or from a substance so common (like a small amount of sugar) that it cannot have any appreciable effects on the condition being treated. It is only when the real drug is significantly more effective than the placebo that its power to treat can be properly attributed to a chemical effect. Today, the term placebo is used to describe any dummy treatment that is used to manipulate a patient's expectations.

The administration of placebos has resulted in at least some improvement with respect to a surprisingly wide range of medical problems. These include dental pain, asthma, multiple sclerosis, the common cold, diabetes, ulcers and Parkinson's disease. Even surgical procedures may owe some of their impact to placebo effects. There have been studies comparing genuine surgery with sham surgery during which patients were anaesthetized and an incision made, but no operation was performed. In one such study, patients suffering from angina, who were given a placebo operation, obtained as much relief as those who underwent genuine heart surgery.

If expectations can influence the symptoms of cardiovascular disease, then clearly expectations can affect the symptoms of psychological problems such as anxiety and depression. The healing setting is, without doubt, an important 'theatrical' device for encouraging positive expectations.

Frank's third common factor is the provision of a rationale, a conceptual scheme – or myth – that provides a plausible explanation for the patient's symptoms and suggests a ritual or procedure for resolving them. Frank points out that any rationale (for any activity) is only plausible to the extent that it is congruent with the dominant beliefs of a host culture. For example, in the middle ages, therapeutic symbols drew their power from association with Christianity. In the contemporary western world, science is invested with the same power. Subsequently, psychotherapists have always been keen to draw attention to their scientific pedigree. Freud promoted himself as an empiricist, fraternized with Einstein and even hoped to win the Nobel Prize. Behaviour therapy is built on foundations laid by Pavlov and Skinner, while cognitive therapy has borrowed a vocabulary from computer studies.

Science can also strengthen what is sometimes called the *Rumpelstiltskin effect.* In the famous fairy story by the brothers Grimm, a queen breaks a wicked dwarf's power over her by guessing his name. This is a very primitive idea that has re-emerged in many different contexts and cultures throughout history. For example, students of black magic once believed that discovering a demon's name would offer protection against his powers. Psychologists and psychiatrists can name the wicked dwarves and demons responsible for mental illness. They have, at their disposal, complex diagnostic systems that have been developed under the reassuring patronage of the scientific establishment. Moreover, once a diagnosis has been made, it will suggest a particular form of treatment. The patient is comforted by the fact that his or her problem has been encountered before, and the practitioner's recognition of the problem immediately suggests knowledge of a treatment strategy.

Frank's final common factor concerns the actual techniques employed to treat psychological problems. He suggests that all forms of psychotherapy employ a 'ritual' or 'procedure' that requires the active participation of both patient and therapist and that is believed to be the means of restoring the patient's health. This ritual might involve lying down on a chaise longue and free-associating (as in psychoanalysis) or learning relaxation procedures (as in behaviour therapy). The exact content of the procedure is unimportant; it is the participation of therapist and patient and their combined belief in the procedure that is the precipitant of change.

Frank points out that every culture has its healing ceremonies, and that all appear to have equal potency. The African witch doctor and Tibetan lama are both able to treat 'mental illness'. Their ability to do so may be no better or worse than the psychoanalyst or cognitive therapist. Moreover, the history of medicine shows that any credible therapeutic procedure, applied in a socially sanctioned manner or setting, will result in at least some improvement.

Although Frank's observations are profoundly insightful, they are, alas, not entirely accurate. Research is beginning to show that certain forms of psychotherapy produce better results when used to treat some problems rather than others. As such, to suggest that all forms of psychotherapy are equivalent is probably incorrect. There can be little doubt that many forms of psychotherapy share a common quantum of efficacy as Frank suggests. Moreover, this is very probably attributable to the four non-specific factors that he identifies; however, the specific elements of any given therapeutic approach may well carry an additive advantage, depending on the nature of the problem being treated.

Irrespective of minor inaccuracies, Frank's *Persuasion and Healing* is a landmark publication. His work has been highly influential, inspiring generations of therapists to view their discipline not as an unhappy coalition of disparate factions, but rather as an integrated whole. The blurring of the boundaries that separate one school of psychotherapy from another has made eclecticism more acceptable. Borrowing a technique from one approach, and using it within the overall framework of another, has become increasingly common in recent years.

The movement for psychotherapy integration is particularly associated with the names of Marvin Goldfried and Paul Wachtel, who, during the 1980s, urged fellow psychotherapists to find common principles and complementary treatment methods. Although they are credited with launching the psychotherapy integration movement, the process had already been under way for many years. Jerome Frank had, of course, already described his four non-specific factors, and cognitive therapy (which is really an agglomeration of humanistic ideas and techniques) was firmly established. Goldfried and Wachtel were significant, insofar as they made 'integration' an explicit objective. Moreover, they were happy to 'speak out' in defence of integration, a stance that a generally partisan profession had been reluctant to publicly endorse.

The convergence of humanistic ideas in the form of cognitive therapy, and the later fusion of cognitive and behavioural approaches, do not require a massive effort of imagination. It is relatively easy to see how these different strands might be brought together in a single weave; however, with the 1977 publication of *Psychoanalysis and Behaviour Therapy: Toward an Integration*, Wachtel attempted to bridge a very deep divide indeed. In this book, he suggested that behavioural techniques, such as the use of homework assignments and imaginal exposure, might be recruited to assist with the exploration of themes pertinent to psychoanalysis. Although the pairing of behaviourism and psychoanalysis might seem, at first glance, to be a doomed marriage, Wachtel was by no means the first to consider how the two approaches might complement each other. There have been both explicit and accidental conflations of behavioural and psychoanalytic ideas since the 1940s. Attempts to straddle these warring camps have rarely proved popular; however, this says far more about the traditional enmity between psychoanalysis and behaviourism than the basic incompatibility of the two approaches.

For example, O. H. Mowrer's two-factor theory of the acquisition and maintenance of anxiety (a linchpin of behaviour therapy) has much in common with the psychoanalytic defence of *suppression*. This defence differs from repression, insofar as unwanted thoughts and memories are purposely (rather than involuntarily) kept out of awareness. In two-factor theory, phobic anxiety is understood to be a classically conditioned response to an innocuous stimulus; however, anxiety is maintained because of avoidance. When a phobic individual approaches a feared situation or object, anxiety rises. When the same individual retreats, anxiety subsides. Avoidance is therefore a defence against anxiety, a kind of behavioural enactment of suppression. In both behaviour therapy and psychoanalysis, the recommended treatment will be some kind of confrontation. The feared object, situation, thought or memory is each ultimately faced, directly. The individual comes to terms with his or her fears, thus rendering either avoidance or suppression unnecessary.

In 1960, Thomas Stampfl developed *Implosion Therapy*, a treatment procedure that is supposed to be psychoanalytic. The patient is instructed to form mental images of feared objects and situations; however, these images are placed in the context of a nightmarish story in which the most distressing features of the feared objects or situations are grossly exaggerated. For example, an individual with a fear of snakes might be guided through a horrific fantasy, in which a giant boa constrictor wraps itself around his or her body, opens its mouth wide and swallows the person whole. Each sensation is explored and discussed in gory detail. The themes and feelings that emerge are thought to reveal underlying sexual and aggressive conflicts – highly relevant material for the psychoanalyst. Nevertheless, the procedure itself is almost identical to behavioural techniques such as imaginal exposure and flooding.

Cognitive analytic therapy (CAT), was originally developed by Anthony Ryle in the 1970s, and is perhaps one of the better known and more successful explicit attempts at integration. Ryle's interest in combining different approaches began when he employed Kelly's repertory grid technique to study the characteristics of patients undergoing psychoanalysis. In CAT, Oedipal themes are still recognized, as are many concepts borrowed from the object relations school. Moreover, as in traditional psychoanalysis, the relationship between therapist and patient is viewed as a valuable source of information and an instrument of change; however, CAT is far more structured than psychoanalysis. The number of sessions is usually limited and certain goals must be achieved before progressing. In addition, once insight into a problem has been gained, behavioural programmes, role-play and written exercises are then employed to make sure that the patient progresses. This is quite different from traditional psychoanalysis, in which insight alone is considered sufficient to produce changes in thinking and behaviour.

It is surprising that, given a recent groundswell of interest in integrative approaches to treatment, CAT has not achieved greater popularity. One explanation might be Ryle's use of overly complex language. For example, he uses the terms *Target Problem* (for what is wrong), Target Problem Procedure (for mental and behavioural factors that maintain the problem), and the *Repertoire of Reciprocal Roles* (to describe patterns of social behaviour established in early childhood). A complete pictorial representation of how problem procedures are generated, connected and maintained is captured is the *procedural sequence object relations model diagram*. Clearly, the frequent use of such technical language makes few concessions to the interested reader.

A more approachable form of integrative therapy is *schema focused cognitive therapy* (SFCT). As the name suggests, it is the invention of one of Beck's acolytes, Jeff Young. SFCT is very much a product of the 1990s and reflects increasing interest in the treatment of 'personality disorders'. A personality disorder is characterized by a long-standing disposition to think and act in a self-defeating way. It is usually associated with impaired social functioning and the frequent experience of inappropriate or extreme emotions. Although SFCT was developed primarily to treat patients with personality disorders, it has implications for the treatment of all psychological problems.

Young has developed his approach within the general framework espoused by Beck; however, Young is far more willing to accommodate within that framework ideas usually found in the psychoanalytic literature. For example, he stresses the importance of very early learning experiences on adult mental health. As such, he might be considered a latter-day Bowlby, or even Klein.

According to Young, there are five basic tasks associated with healthy infant development. Firstly, the establishment of *autonomy*. A child must learn to function independently, without excessive help from his or her parents. Secondly, *connectedness*. A child must learn to be comfortable with, and feel understood by others. Thirdly, *competence*. A child must become confident that certain skills and abilities have been successfully acquired. Fourthly, a child must develop *reasonable expectations of others*. Finally, a child must learn to respect his or her own *realistic limits* (for example, being neither too self-sacrificing nor too selfish).

When child-rearing practices and the social environment are good, the five tasks are (each to a greater or lesser extent) successfully accomplished; however, when child-rearing patterns are inadequate or disturbed, the child will be unable to accomplish one or more of the five tasks. This will have a lasting effect on the child's development. For example, an overprotective parent may prevent a child from achieving autonomy. Such a parent might repeatedly 'help' his or her child, even when the child is experiencing minimal difficulty. The child is never given enough responsibility and may feel inadequate when left to his or her own devices. This general feeling of inadequacy may persist into adulthood, particularly when separated from others. Even when left alone for a short period of time, the individual who has never accomplished autonomy will begin to feel uncomfortable and experience thoughts like 'I can't cope' or 'I need someone to be here'.

These unpleasant thoughts and feelings are ascribed to the presence of an early maladaptive schema (EMS), Young's principal addition to the traditional cognitive model.

Beck uses the term schema to describe mental structures that organize information in memory and influence perception. In traditional cognitive therapy, schemas are largely comprised of related beliefs. Although Young uses the same term as Beck, the former's conception is somewhat different. An EMS is not readily reducible to propositions or beliefs and resembles something more like a role or stance. An EMS develops as a result of unsatisfactory relationships formed with parents (and possibly peers) during the first few years of life; because EMSs develop in early childhood – mostly by the end of the third year – they may be largely non-verbal. The script, as it were, contains directions, but few words.

Once an EMS is established, it will serve as a template for understanding and responding to the world, particularly with respect to social situations. EMSs and traditional Beckian schemas can operate in the same person; however, the EMS will be the more important determinant of self-defeating behaviour. Like traditional schemas, EMSs will be activated by events and situations that resonate with specific features of the EMS. So, as in the example cited above, the individual who has developed an early dependency schema will react badly when asked by a partner or friend to tolerate even short periods of autonomy. Failure to accomplish any one of Young's five tasks can result in the development of one or more EMSs.

When an ordinary schema is activated, this will result in the occurrence of many negative automatic thoughts. The same is also true of an EMS; however, an activated EMS is more likely to produce distressing physical changes (such as increased heart rate or nausea) and waves of intense feelings.

EMSs provide an explanation for why it is that certain painful experiences in childhood are often repeated in adulthood. It is an extraordinary fact, confirmed by generations of clinical observation, that many individuals have a marked tendency to recreate painful childhood experiences throughout their adult life. For example, the woman with an overprotective mother will report a history of relationships with overprotective men.

The boy who tried to impress an indifferent father becomes the ambitious man seeking the attentions of a largely indifferent world (and so on).

Young suggests that patterns of self-defeating behaviour are preserved by underlying EMSs; however, the EMS is also a fundamental aspect of an affected individual's personality. Subsequently, attempts to modify an EMS in therapy will be met with considerable resistance. Although an individual's self-defeating behaviour might be the cause of much distress, it is at least familiar. Relinquishing well-practised behavioural and emotional routines can be associated with terrible anxiety. The ensuing experience could be compared with what an actor might suffer if forced to perform on stage without having had an adequate opportunity to learn his script. Even an unsatisfactory role would feel more comfortable than the insecurity and uncertainty of being so lamentably unprepared.

Given that relinquishing or modifying an EMS will be associated with extreme anxiety, cognitive mechanisms may evolve that serve to preserve the EMS (and associated patterns of behaviour). For example, an individual might be able to justify a self-defeating pattern of behaviour; however, such justifications might depend on a considerable amount of bias and distortion. Here, Young is accomplishing a seamless fusion of ideas drawn from psychoanalysis and cognitive therapy. Anxiety is being reduced by a defence, which, on closer examination, proves to be comprised of Beck's thinking errors. In Young's approach, negative automatic thoughts (which distort experience) help to preserve the EMS. Other 'defences' are described by Young, most notably 'avoidance' and 'compensation' (which is really a re-statement of Adlerian 'overcompensation').

The practice of SFCT is truly synthetic. Young advocates use of the relationship between therapist and patient as a source of information, thus recognizing the importance of the psychoanalytic idea of transference. He makes considerable use of cognitive therapy techniques, particularly the challenging of unhelpful thoughts and beliefs, and recommends behavioural homework assignments (such as exposure). Young has even revived some of the experiential or emotive techniques devised by Fritz Perls (such as the empty chair). These are used to trigger or activate EMSs in the therapy session.

CAT and SFCT are particularly good examples of integrative psychotherapy. They represent the growing awareness among psychotherapists that many key ideas are ubiquitous, surfacing and resurfacing in different schools. It is as though psychotherapy is edging towards a unified account of itself – what might be described as a *metapsychology* of suffering and its treatment. When this process is complete, psychotherapy may have matured to the extent that its basic and common principles can be described with some precision. This is a very welcome prospect, and one that Freud, with his aspirations for scientific recognition, would have probably relished.

In 1910, at a medical congress in Hamburg, an eminent professor interrupted a debate in which Freud's ideas were raised by banging his fist on a table and shouting: 'This is not a topic for discussion at a scientific meeting: it is a matter for the police.' In 1958, Hans Eysenck attempted to introduce the topic of behaviour therapy to the psychiatric establishment in Britain and was very nearly assaulted when the audience expressed its disapproval by rioting. Given that psychotherapy has always had to struggle for recognition, it is curious that psychotherapists have been slow to recognize the advantages of showing the world a united front. The 'natural and justifiable differences' between the various schools have been thoroughly overemphasized – mostly for political reasons – giving the impression that there is little in psychotherapy that can be readily agreed upon. This is most regrettable, because psychotherapy has never been short of critics.

One of the most scurrilous attacks on psychotherapy in recent years was – ironically – orchestrated by a disillusioned psychotherapist, Jeffrey Masson. In the preface to his much vaunted diatribe, *Against Therapy* (first published in 1988), he suggests: 'the very idea of psychotherapy is wrong. The structure of psychotherapy is such that no matter how kindly a person is, when that person becomes a therapist, he or she is engaged in acts that are bound to diminish the dignity, autonomy, and freedom of the person who comes for help.'

To support his thesis, Masson collects together the most extraordinary body of material. He points out that some of the key figures in psychotherapy, such as Freud and Jung, were far from saintly. Moreover, many of their ideas were misconceived and incorrect. This much would have been readily accepted fifty years ago. He then, however, catalogues some of the most extreme examples of abuse that have ever masqueraded under the banner of psychotherapy. An example is the *direct analysis* of the now almost totally forgotten John Rosen. Masson describes the $5,000 dollar a month treatment of a woman called Sally Zinman in 1971: 'Without a word of explanation, he and his main aide, an ex-Marine, tore off all her clothes except her underpants and began beating her on the face and breasts (the aide held her down while Rosen beat her). She was then tied to her bed, still with no clothes on, and kept that way for twenty-four hours, under close guard.' Such examples are hardly representative of the everyday practice of psychotherapy! They serve only to frighten the general public and mislead. One might just as well judge the value of medicine by examining the murderous behaviour of Dr Crippen.

For the average person, the fact that some unscrupulous therapists have been known to abuse their patients is less important than the issue of whether or not psychotherapy works. Masson dismisses the question of efficacy in a single line: 'The value of psychotherapy cannot be decided by statistics.' However, for an individual in psychological distress, the degree to which psychotherapy can ameliorate suffering will be the gold standard by which it is judged.

A worrying aspect of Masson's work is his almost complete ignorance of the major developments in psychotherapy over the last fifty years. Moreover, although he is happy to condemn the practice of psychotherapy, he has nothing to offer in its place. If psychotherapy were abandoned, as Masson suggests, then it is doubtful that those who are most in need of help would approve. The millions of individuals suffering from anxiety disorders and depression would not appreciate being denied treatment, on the grounds that they were being spared the indignity of entering into a relationship characterized by a power imbalance. Finally, to reject psychotherapy because it might involve one person depending on another is somewhat weak; society is nothing if not a coalition of mutually beneficial dependencies. In the words of the poet John Donne: 'No man is an island.'

Although Masson's critique captured the attention of a large international audience, psychotherapy weathered the sub-sequent storm of media interest relatively unscathed; however, the legitimacy of psychotherapy was soon to be called into question again, when a new family of antidepressant drugs – known as the SSRIs – gave biological psychiatry a new lease of life.

Ever since the discovery that mental illness could be caused by syphilis, the fortunes of biological psychiatry have waxed and waned. Nevertheless, every decade since the 1950s has marked an awesome advance in the understanding of brain chemistry. Moreover, each of these advances has led to the development of more effective forms of medication. The SSRIs seemed to be remarkably potent. Indeed, many biological psychiatrists began to suggest that, in the very near future, all psychological problems would yield to a chemical analysis. Psychotherapy, in its various forms and guises, would shortly become a footnote in the history of medicine. In the age of the SSRI, 'natural and justifiable differences' had become a luxury psychotherapists could ill-afford.

One SSRI, more than any other, is responsible for the recent rhetoric of biological psychiatrists. Fluoxetine hydrochloride, better known by its trade name Prozac, became a favourite within the medical community more swiftly than any other psychoactive drug in the history of pharmacology. This was largely because, over a relatively short time, clinical observations suggested that Prozac possessed some remarkable properties. Peter Kramer, the psychiatrist and author of *Listening to Prozac*, wrote of patients who became 'better than well'. Individuals suffering from depression claimed that Prozac not only restored them to prior levels of intellectual and emotional functioning, but also actually improved on these. Kramer's patients became energetic, lively and 'socially attractive'. To describe this effect Kramer coined the term *cosmetic psychopharmacology*.

These original clinical observations and subsequent media

coverage inspired ordinary people, with no history of mental illness, to request Prozac on prescription. This was a curious response from a public generally apprehensive about the potential side effects (and addictive properties) of drugs that act on the mind. Kramer wrote about a 'subset' of 'fairly healthy people who show dramatic good responses to Prozac; people who are not so much cured of illness as transformed'. Prozac was being used, not as an antidepressant (the use for which it was developed), but rather a 'thymoleptic', that is, a drug that alters personality. Eventually, the green and off-white capsule displaced starlets and politicians on the cover of *Newsweek*. Prozac was not only a designer drug, it was also a celebrity.

Much of the information circulated about Prozac is transparent propaganda. It is certainly an effective drug, but it is not a panacea. Moreover, there are few professionals who would now subscribe to the view that it is a genuine thymoleptic. Prozac can indeed alter mood, but it will not transform a lifelong authoritarian into a liberal. Nevertheless, its power to change (at least some) minds has inspired a timely debate.

The rhetoric of biological psychiatrists concerning the imminent demise of psychotherapy was, and always has been, somewhat misleading. In spite of Prozac's success, current knowledge of brain chemistry is far from complete. Subsequently, many forms of mental illness will remain untreatable using medication in the foreseeable future. A few of these untreatable cases, respond well to psychotherapy. Even Kramer, who is more than willing to extol the virtues of medication, is a keen advocate of psychotherapy when symptoms are not too severe. Indeed, he describes it as 'the single most helpful technology for the treatment of minor depression and anxiety'. However, it is not inconceivable that, at some point in the future, drugs will be developed that really can treat all forms of mental illness. Even Freud thought this inevitable. Would it be desirable to eradicate human suffering completely? What would the long-term consequences be for a culture that had disposed of sorrow, anguish and fear?

Aldous Huxley provides an answer in *Brave New World*. In his dystopian vision of the future, one of the key weapons used to combat unhappiness is 'soma', a drug that will neutralize any unpleasant emotions. Huxley's principal protagonists are unable to tolerate suffering of any kind. In such a world, life becomes vapid and banal. There is no place for high art or unrequited love, truth or beauty. These things become meaningless. Only the empty pursuit of superficial pleasures is permitted. The methods that humanity endorses with respect to the management of suffering have ramifications that extend well beyond the practice of medicine.

If the capacity to suffer is removed from the sphere of human experience, then something essential is lost. We cease to be human, or at least, human as the term is currently understood. Dostoyevsky perceived suffering, not merely as pain, but as an ennobling and elevating influence: 'There is only one thing that I dread: not to be worthy of my sufferings,' he once wrote: This is a sentiment shared by Viktor Frankl, an individual eminently qualified to comment on these matters: 'If there is meaning in life at all, then there must be a meaning in suffering. Suffering is an ineradicable part of life, even as fate and death. Without suffering and death human life cannot be complete.'

It was suggested earlier that the gold standard by which any treatment is judged is its effectiveness; however, all interventions have certain costs. The ultimate cost of biological psychiatry may be the most valued possession of humanity: *humanity itself*. This is a cost that many are reluctant to pay. The talking cure is a human solution to the problems of suffering. Psychotherapy distinguishes pain with meaning and purpose. Sadness and fear are understood to be, not rogue emotions, but part of the human condition.

This book started with the Buddha's observation that 'All life is suffering'. The Buddhist solution to that suffering is liberation through non-attachment, the gradual severing of links with the world. This view is, of course, common to many spiritual belief systems. Psychotherapy is, in many ways, the exact opposite; the solution to suffering is the formation of a temporary, but meaningful attachment. This is very revealing with respect to the fundamental social nature of humanity. The secular response to suffering is to use each other in the face of adversity. Intimacy is placed in the service of healing. Language (Jones' contemporary equivalent of grooming) is used to evoke a sense of primal security. In a post-Copernican and Darwinian universe, human beings are learning to value the curative power of relationships.

John Bowlby suggested that a strong emotional bond with a parent is essential if a child is to grow up feeling secure. When a child is separated from a parent, it experiences separation anxiety and may show a separation protest, for example, crying, screaming, shouting, biting and kicking. It is thought that the separation protest is a normal response, and represents an attempt to restore the attachment bond, and by punishing the care-giver, prevents further separation. The human race has been separated from its attachment figure. Copernicus and Darwin have obliterated the old religious certainties. The human race can cry, scream, shout, bite and kick, but for whose benefit? Who, after all, is listening? Perhaps, only each other. And surprisingly, this may prove to be all that we really need.

Further Reading

This book is not meant to be an academic textbook. It is supposed to be an accessible and hopefully entertaining introduction to psychotherapy and the mind; however, for those who wish to delve further into areas covered in each chapter, the following books are highly recommended.

Chapter 1
Breuer, J. and Freud, S. (1991) *Studies on Hysteria*. The Penguin Freud Library (Edited by Angela Richards). Harmondsworth: Penguin.
Gay, P. (1988) *Freud: A Life for Our Time*. London: J. M. Dent & Sons.
Showalter, E. (1987) *The Female Malady: Women, Madness and English Culture, 1830–1980*. London: Virago.
Zilboorg, G. and Henry, G. W. (1941) *A History of Medical Psychology*. New York: Norton.

Chapter 2
Gay, P. (1988) *Freud: A Life for Our Time*. London: J. M. Dent & Sons.
Freud, S. (1991) The *Interpretation of Dreams*. The Penguin Freud Library (Edited by Angela Richards). Harmondsworth: Penguin.
Freud, S. (1991) *On Metapsychology*. The Penguin Freud Library (Edited by Angela Richards). Harmondsworth: Penguin.
Stafford-Clark, D. (1967) *What Freud Really Said*. Harmondsworth: Penguin.

Chapter 3
Brown, J. A. C. (1964) *Freud and the Post-Freudians*. Harmondsworth: Penguin.
Berne, E. (1964) *The Games People Play*. Harmondsworth: Penguin.
Freud, S. and Jung, C. G. (1991) *The Freud/Jung Letters*. Harmondsworth: Penguin.

Gay, P. (1988) *Freud: A Life for Our Time.* London: J. M. Dent & Sons.

Holmes, J. (1993) *John Bowlby and Attachment Theory.* London: Routledge.

Chapter 4

Davison, G. C. and Neale, J. M. (1982) *Abnormal Psychology: An Experimental and Clinical Approach.* New York: John Wiley & Sons.

Fancher, R. E. (1990) *Pioneers of Psychology* (Second edition). London: Norton.

Kevles, D. J. (1985) *In the Name of Eugenics: Genetics and the Uses of Human Heredity.* Harmondsworth: Penguin.

Chapter 5

Clarkson, P. and Mackewn, J. (1993) *Fritz Perls.* London: Sage.

Frankl, V. E. (1985) *Man's Search for Meaning* (Revised and updated). New York: Washington Square Press.

Kelly, G. (1955) *The Psychology of Personal Constructs.* New York: Norton (Reprinted by Routledge, 1990).

Nelson-Jones, R. (1995) *The Theory and Practice of Counselling.* London: Cassell.

Rogers, C. R. (1967) *On Becoming a Person: A Therapist's View of Psychotherapy.* London: Constable.

Chapter 6

Beck, A. T. (1989) *Cognitive Therapy and the Emotional Disorders.* Harmondsworth: Penguin.

Weishaar, M. E. (1993) *Aaron T. Beck.* London: Sage.

Chapter 7

Frank, J. D. and Frank, J. (1993) *Persuasion and Healing: A Comparative Study of Psychotherapy* (Third edition). Baltimore and London: Johns Hopkins University Press.

Kramer, P. D. (1994) *Listening to Prozac.* London: Fourth Estate.

Masson, J. (1993) *Against Therapy.* London: HarperCollins.

Ryle, A. (1995) *Cognitive Analytic Therapy: Developments in Theory and Practice.* Chichester: John Wiley & Sons.

Young, J. E. and Klosko, J. S. (1993) *Reinventing Your Life.* New York: Plume.

Index

Adler, Alfred 48, 49–52, 62, 68, 73, 75, 127, 146
Anna O. *see* Pappenheim, Bertha
aversion therapy 100–1, 102
Bandura, Albert 135
Bartlett, Sir Frederic 121–2
Beck, Aaron 131–4, 137–42, 144–6, 149, 160, 161, 162
behaviour modification 136–7
behaviourism 84–105, 128, 134–7, 143, 147, 148–9, 154, 156, 158–9, 164
Berne, Eric 70–3, 153
Bioenergetic school 73–4
Bowlby, John 65–70, 73, 75, 132, 161, 169
Breuer, Dr Joseph 10–17, 20, 41–2, 138, 148, 150, 153
Charcot, Jean-Martin 10–11, 13
classical conditioning 80–3, 86–7, 90, 134–5, 159
cognitive behaviour therapy 136–7, 146
cognitive therapy 137–46, 156, 158, 163
compensation 49–52
conditioning 80–3, 86–7, 88–90, 93–7, 102, 134–5, 159
Copernicus, Nicholas 2–3, 18, 20–1, 22, 42–3, 169
Darwin, Charles 3–4, 17, 20–1, 22, 43, 103–4, 169
defence mechanisms 30, 34, 116–17
dream interpretation 18–19, 39–41, 42, 51, 60
drugs 151, 166–8; placebos 155–6
Elektra complex 33, 34, 36, 41–4, 55
Ellis, Albert 124–7, 133, 139, 140, 142, 145
EMS (early maladaptive schema) 162–3
eugenics 103–5
Eysenck, Hans 92–3, 95, 164
flooding 96, 97, 101, 159
Frank, Jerome, 151–8
Frankl, Viktor 106–10, 118, 119, 137, 168
free association 16, 18, 38–9, 42, 127, 133
Freud, Anna 43–4, 45, 62, 65, 151
Freud, Sigmund 13–23, 24–46, 47–8, 153, 158, 164, 165, 167; and Adler 49, 50–2; and Beck 144–6, 149; and behaviourism 83, 92, 100; and Berne 70; and biological determinism 21–2; and Bowlby 66–7; and Breuer 10–11, 14–17, 20, 150; consciousness levels 28–9; cultural significance of 24–6, 76–7, 147–8; death 45–6; and dream interpretation 18–19, 39–42; and humanistic psychology 114, 117, 123, 125, 128; id, ego and superego 29–30, 34, 36–8, 54–5, 62, 125; and infant sexuality 17–18, 20, 31–4; instincts and drives 27–8; and Jung 52–5, 58–9, 61; and Klein 64–5; and post-Freudians 74–7, 146–8; *see also* Oedipus complex; psychoanalytic movement
Freudian slips 39
Fromm, Erich 52, 74
gestalt therapy 109–13, 118
humanistic psychology 109–20, 147, 148, 149, 152
hypnotism 10, 13–14, 18
hysteria 10–11, 12–17, 20, 42–3
implosion therapy 159
Jung, Carl Gustav 48, 49, 50, 52–61, 68, 73, 75, 76, 115, 146, 165
Kelly, George 118–21, 123–4, 132, 143, 160
Klein, Melanie 62–5, 66, 68, 73, 74, 75, 129, 146–7, 151, 161
logotherapy 108–10
Masson, Jeffrey 164–5
maternal deprivation 66–8, 132
modelling 135
Mowrer, O.H. 88–9, 159
natural selection 3–4, 103–4
negative automatic thoughts (NATs) 133, 139–42
Nordau, Max 104–5
object relations 63, 160
Oedipus complex 19–20, 32–4, 35–6, 37, 43, 50, 55, 59, 160
operant conditioning 89–90
Pappenheim, Bertha (Anna O.) 14–15, 16–17, 41–2, 148
Pavlov, I.P. 78–84, 87, 90, 93, 101, 156
Perls, Fritz 109–13, 118, 128, 164
personal construct psychology (PCP) 118–21
psychoanalytic movement 47–77, 92–3, 128, 132, 146–9, 158–9; *see also* Freud, Sigmund
regression 37, 59
Reich, William 73–4
repression 13, 30, 36
RET (rational emotive therapy) 124–7, 145
Rogers, Carl 113–18, 126, 139, 140, 152
schemas/schemata 121–3, 140–2, 162–3
sex therapy 97–8, 101
SFCT (schema focused cognitive therapy) 160–4
Skinner, B.F. 90–1, 99, 101–2, 135, 156
Socratic questioning 143, 144
Studies on Hysteria (Freud and Breuer) 14–16, 22–3, 24, 138, 150
systematic desensitization 94–7, 98
therapeutic relationship 41–2, 59–60, 98, 114, 115, 118, 142–3, 152–5
token economy programmes 99–100, 101
transactional analysis (TA) 70–3
transference 41–2
unconscious 18, 20, 21, 28, 38, 43, 54; collective 55–6, 75
Watson, J.B. 84–8, 89, 91, 93, 99, 103, 134
Wolpe, Joseph 93–5, 96, 97, 138